✧ *Companions for the Journey* ✧

Praying with
Martin Luther

✧ *Companions for the Journey* ✧

Praying with
Martin Luther

by
Peter E. Bastien

Saint Mary's Press
Christian Brothers Publications
Winona, Minnesota

To the Women of my life:
✧ *My mother, Whilhelmina (Mae)* ✧
My wife, Pat
My daughters, Florence and Sarah

Genuine recycled paper with 10% post-consumer waste.
Printed with soy-based ink.

The publishing team for this book included Carl Koch, series editor; Mary Duerson, copy editor; James H. Gurley, production editor; Cindi Ramm, designer; Sam Thiewes, illustrator; pre-press, printing, and binding by the graphics division of Saint Mary's Press.

The acknowledgments continue on page 130.

Printed in the United States of America

Printing: 9 8 7 6 5 4 3 2 1

Year: 2007 06 05 04 03 02 01 00 99

ISBN 0-88489-580-7

✧ Contents ✧

✧ Foreword ✧

Companions for the Journey

Just as food is required for human life, so are companions. Indeed, the word *companions* comes from two Latin words: *com*, meaning "with," and *panis*, meaning "bread." Companions nourish our heart, mind, soul, and body. They are also the people with whom we can celebrate the sharing of bread.

Perhaps the most touching stories in the Bible are about companionship: the Last Supper, the wedding feast at Cana, the sharing of the loaves and the fishes, and Jesus' breaking of bread with the disciples on the road to Emmaus. Each incident of companionship with Jesus revealed more about his mercy, love, wisdom, suffering, and hope. When Jesus went to pray in the Garden of Olives, he craved the companionship of the Apostles. They let him down. But God sent the Spirit to inflame the hearts of the Apostles, and they became faithful companions to Jesus and to one another.

Throughout history, other faithful companions have followed Jesus and the Apostles. These saints and mystics have also taken the journey from conversion, through suffering, to resurrection. Just as they were inspired by the holy people who went before them, so too may you be inspired by these saints and mystics and take them as your companions on your spiritual journey.

The Companions for the Journey series is a response to the spiritual hunger of Christians. This series makes available the rich spiritual teachings of mystics and guides whose wisdom can help us on our pilgrimage. As you complete the last meditation in each volume, it is hoped that you will feel supported, challenged, and affirmed by a soul-companion on your spiritual journey.

The spiritual hunger that has emerged over the last twenty years is a great sign of renewal in Christian life. People fill retreat programs and workshops on topics in spirituality. The demand for spiritual directors exceeds the number available. Interest in the lives and writings of saints and mystics is increasing as people search for models of whole and holy Christian life.

Praying with Martin Luther

Praying with Martin Luther is more than just a book about Martin's spirituality. This book seeks to engage you in praying in the way that Martin did about issues and themes that were central to his experience. Each meditation can enlighten your understanding of his spirituality and lead you to reflect on your own experience.

The goal of *Praying with Martin Luther* is that you will discover Martin's rich spirituality and integrate his spirit and wisdom into your relationship with God, with your brothers and sisters, and with your own heart and mind.

Suggestions for Praying with Martin Luther

Meet Martin Luther, a fascinating companion for your pilgrimage, by reading the introduction to this book. It provides a brief biography of Martin and an outline of the major themes of his spirituality.

Once you meet Martin Luther, you will be ready to pray with him and to encounter God, your sisters and brothers, and yourself in new and wonderful ways. To help your prayer, here are some suggestions that have been part of the tradition of Christian spirituality:

Create a sacred space. Jesus said, "'Whenever you pray, go into your room and shut the door and pray to your [God] who is in secret; and your [God] who sees in secret will reward you'" (Matthew 6:6). Solitary prayer is best done in a place where you can have privacy and silence, both of which can be luxuries in the life of busy people. If privacy and silence are not possible, create a quiet, safe place within yourself, perhaps while riding to and from work, while sitting in line at the dentist's office, or while waiting for someone. Do the best you can, knowing that a loving God is present everywhere. Whether the meditations in this book are used for solitary prayer or with a group, try to create a prayerful mood with candles, meditative music, an open Bible, or a crucifix.

Open yourself to the power of prayer. Every human experience has a religious dimension. All of life is suffused with God's presence. So remind yourself that God is present as you begin your period of prayer. Do not worry about distractions. If something keeps intruding during your prayer, spend some time talking with God about it. Be flexible because God's spirit blows where it will.

Prayer can open your mind and widen your vision. Be open to new ways of seeing God, people, and yourself. As you open yourself to the spirit of God, different emotions are evoked, such as sadness from tender memories, or joy from a celebration recalled. Our emotions are messages from God that can tell us much about our spiritual quest. Also, prayer strengthens our will to act. Through prayer, God can touch our will and empower us to live according to what we know is true.

Finally, many of the meditations in this book will call you to employ your memories, your imagination, and the circumstances of your life as subjects for prayer. The great mystics and saints realized that they had to use all their resources to know God better. Indeed, God speaks to us continually and touches us constantly. We must learn to listen and feel with all the means that God has given us.

Come to prayer with an open mind, heart, and will.

Preview each meditation before beginning. After you have placed yourself in God's presence, spend a few moments previewing the readings and especially the reflection activities. Several reflection activities are given in each meditation because different styles of prayer appeal to different personalities

or personal needs. **Note that each meditation has more reflection activities than can be done during one prayer period.
Therefore, select only one or two reflection activities each
time you use a meditation. Do not feel compelled to complete all the reflection activities.**

Read meditatively. Each meditation offers you a story
about Martin and a reading from his writings. Take your time
reading. If a particular phrase touches you, stay with it. Relish
its feelings, meanings, and concerns.

Use the reflections. Following the readings is a short reflection in commentary form, which is meant to give perspec-
tive to the readings. Then you are offered several ways of
meditating on the readings and the theme of the prayer. You
may be familiar with the different methods of meditating, but
in case you are not, they are described briefly here:

✦ *Repeated short prayer or mantra:* One means of focusing your
   prayer is to use a *mantra,* or "prayer word." The mantra
   may be a single word or a short phrase taken from the
   readings or from the Scriptures. For example, a short prayer for meditation 2 in this book might simply be "Christ for
   me." Repeated slowly in harmony with your breathing, the
   mantra helps you center your heart and mind on one action
   or attribute of God.

✦ *Lectio divina:* This type of meditation is "divine studying,"
   a concentrated reflection on the word of God or the wisdom of a spiritual writer. Most often in *lectio divina,* you will
   be invited to read one of the passages several times and
   then concentrate on one or two sentences, pondering their
   meaning for you and their effect on you. *Lectio divina* commonly ends with formulation of a resolution.

✦ *Guided meditation:* In this type of meditation, our imagination helps us consider alternative actions and likely consequences. Our imagination helps us experience new ways of
   seeing God, our neighbors, ourselves, and nature. When
   Jesus told his followers parables and stories, he engaged
   their imagination. In this book, you will be invited to follow
   guided meditations.

One way of doing a guided meditation is to read the scene or story several times, until you know the outline and can recall it when you enter into reflection. Or before your prayer time, you may wish to record the meditation on a tape recorder. If so, remember to allow pauses for reflection between phrases and to speak with a slow, peaceful pace and tone. Then, during prayer, when you have finished the readings and the reflection commentary, you can turn on your recording of the meditation and be led through it. If you find your own voice too distracting, ask a friend to make the tape for you.

✦ *Examen of consciousness:* The reflections often will ask you to examine how God has been speaking to you in your past and present experience—in other words, the reflections will ask you to examine your awareness of God's presence in your life.

✦ *Journal writing:* Writing is a process of discovery. If you write for any length of time, stating honestly what is on your mind and in your heart, you will unearth much about who you are, how you stand with your God, what deep longings reside in your soul, and more. In some reflections, you will be asked to write a dialog with Jesus or someone else. If you have never used writing as a means of meditation, try it. Reserve a special notebook for your journal writing. If desired, you can go back to your entries at a future time for an examen of consciousness.

✦ *Action:* Occasionally, a reflection will suggest singing a favorite hymn, going out for a walk, or undertaking some other physical activity. Actions can be meaningful forms of prayer.

Using the Meditations for Group Prayer

If you wish to use the meditations for community prayer, these suggestions may help:

✦ Read the theme to the group. Call the community into the presence of God, using the short opening prayer. Invite one or two participants to read one or both readings. If you use both readings, observe the pause between them.

✦ The reflection commentary may be used as a reading, or it can be deleted, depending on the needs and interests of the group.

✦ Select one of the reflection activities for your group. Allow sufficient time for your group to reflect, to recite a centering prayer or mantra, to accomplish a studying prayer *(lectio divina)*, or to finish an examen of consciousness. Depending on the group and the amount of available time, you may want to invite the participants to share their reflections, responses, or petitions with the group.

✦ Reading the passage from the Scriptures may serve as a summary of the meditation.

✦ If a formulated prayer or a psalm is given as a closing, it may be recited by the entire group. Or you may ask participants to offer their own prayers for the closing.

Now you are ready to begin praying with Martin Luther, a faithful and caring companion on this stage of your spiritual journey. It is hoped that you will find him to be a true soul-companion.

CARL KOCH,
Editor

✧ **Preface** ✧

There are two kinds of Lutherans in the world. One kind is institutional Lutherans, people who belong to an organized synod (Lutherans use this word as roughly equivalent to diocese) of the Lutheran church. I am a member of the Washington, D.C., Metro Synod of the Evangelical Lutheran Church in America. The other kind is confessional Lutherans, that is, people who share Martin Luther's theological convictions, especially his core belief that the doctrine of justification by grace (alone!) through faith (alone!) is the essence of the Christian faith, leading to a new understanding of who God is and what human life is all about.

Many people, including clergy, who belong to the Lutheran church are not confessionally Lutheran. On the other hand, Martin Luther has many soul mates in every denomination and, if we had eyes to see, probably many even beyond the boundaries of the Christian church.

This book tries to be a practical introduction to Martin's life and thought for people who find themselves in Martin's predicament and for people to whom his journey to God makes sense. Although this is a book on spirituality, it will probably be most helpful to people who have a hard time with spirituality. People who are comfortable with the church, with prayer and spiritual life, will probably wonder what Brother Martin is fussing about. People for whom God is a meaningful presence and a self-evident reality will scratch their heads over Martin Luther. In many respects, Martin is a theologian and pastor for the spiritually bereft. He speaks for those who have existed throughout history and for whom God is lost and life is threatened at its very root. Martin lived and wrote for people who can no longer find God. His Gospel is of a God who came to find us.

✧ Introduction ✧

An "Unworthy Evangelist
of Our Lord Jesus Christ"

For five hundred years, writers have filled library shelves with volumes about Martin Luther. With good reason. The reform that he began shook his world, and, except for Christ's, his effect on the church, society, and thought is probably without parallel. Martin Luther stands as a strong and faithful companion to all Christians, even to Roman Catholics who might still mistakenly consider him an enemy to their beliefs. Martin's reform movement compelled the church of his day to pull itself out of a period of corruption, confusion, and decay. He called all Christians to a renewal of their faith in Christ and dependence on God's grace for salvation.

Upon the celebration of Martin Luther's five hundredth birthday in 1983, the Joint Roman Catholic–Lutheran Commission issued this statement:

> We see on both sides [Roman Catholic and Lutheran] a lessening of outdated, polemically colored images of Luther. He is beginning to be honored in common as a witness to the Gospel, a teacher in the faith, and a herald of spiritual renewal. . . .
>
> As witness to the Gospel, Luther proclaimed the biblical message of God's judgment and grace, of the scandal and the power of the cross, of the lostness of human beings, and of God's act of salvation. As an "unworthy evangelist of our Lord Jesus Christ," Luther points beyond his own person in order to confront us all the more

inescapably with the promise and the claim of the Gospel he confessed. . . .

This new attitude to Luther is reflected in what Cardinal Willebrands said . . . . : "Who . . . would still deny that Martin Luther was a deeply religious person who with honesty and dedication sought for the message of the Gospel? Who would deny that in spite of the fact that he fought against the Roman Catholic Church and the Apostolic See—and for the sake of truth one must not remain silent about this—he retained a considerable part of the old Catholic faith? Indeed, is it not true that the Second Vatican Council has even implemented requests that were first expressed by Martin Luther, among others, as a result of which many aspects of Christian faith and life now find better expression than they did before? To be able to say this in spite of all the differences is a reason for great joy and much hope." (Rusch and Gros, pp. 8–12)

By the 1998 "Joint Declaration on the Doctrine of Justification," the Catholic church and most Lutheran churches had agreed on the use of the Gospel that was so dear to Luther, and confessed that past condemnations on this theme no longer apply to one another.

For the Sake of Truth

Martin Luther lived in an era with close parallels to our own time. Scholars debate whether he was the last of the medievals or the first of the moderns. In many respects, he was both. His world was in the midst of fundamental change. The medieval worldview, its philosophy and spirituality, was losing its coherence. As the ground gave way beneath his feet, Martin struggled to find a way of making sense of life. That is what good theology always does. That is what vital religion always does.

Today, we find ourselves in a time of similar upheaval. One of the designations scholars give to our period is "post-," "post-Christian" and "post-Modern." They mean that human culture has entered a period of drift: we know what we're not, but we still don't know what we are. We are desperately trying to figure out who we are, sometimes with dangerous consequences.

Luther's answers will not necessarily be our answers. He lived in a Eurocentric universe. He knew next to nothing about modern science and didn't like what he did know. The modern study of Scripture was in its infancy. His world was, in many ways, narrow and chauvinistic.

Luther's usefulness starts with his searing honesty both about himself and about his world. He willingly questioned everything for the sake of truth. Where his spirituality explodes with power, even today, is in his insistence that the church address the real questions of real people. Martin Luther saw that the scholastic theology and rigid ritualism of the Middle Ages had grown sterile and divorced from the vast suffering all around him, and within him. Luther wanted nothing to do with a God who remained outside that suffering, and the prevalent belief that God caused suffering made his blood run cold.

When Martin finally encountered Jesus, it was as if he had found a "new God." He found the reality of a gracious love that enters our humanity with all its loss and pain, transfigures humanity through grace, and gives it back to us. Jesus is true God (the Middle Ages was clear about that), but also truly human. We, on the other hand, are not God and must not aspire to be God. We are false humans when our humanity has been distorted and broken by sin: that is, our refusal of the God who is love. Jesus, the true human, shows us the way back to a true humanity. The story of how Brother Martin found Jesus, his "new God," can enlighten our own spiritual journey.

Brother Martin was an "evangelical catholic." Paul Tillich said that Martin was trying to bring Protestant principle and Catholic substance together. Martin sought a middle way between a stubborn, unchanging Catholicism and a revolutionary, destructive Protestantism. Reading Martin's polemical tracts against the Roman church makes him seem to be a "take no prisoners" Protestant, but his tracts against other reformers make him sound like an extremely conservative Catholic.

Reading bits and pieces of Luther's works leads to a warped view of this complex man.

Luther was not trying to jettison our Christian past. He wanted to keep everything that could honestly be kept. His goal was reformation, not a new church. He failed in that goal, as did his opponents, to the detriment of us all and of Christ's mission in the world. If he were alive today, he would most likely take heart in the progress toward Christian unity and renewal.

Early Martin Luther

The day of Martin Luther's birth is known with certainty, but not the year. He was born on 10 November and was baptized on the following day, the feast of Saint Martin of Tours. The year was either 1483 or 1482. His parents were Hans and Margaretha Luder, Ludher, or Luther: all these spellings were used. His ancestors were peasant farmers, but Martin's father had become a copper miner. The Mansfeld region, where the Luther's lived, was a prime mining area. Later, the family moved up into a middle-class position when Hans became a smeltermaster. He served in responsible positions in his community and was, for a time, relatively well-to-do. Martin had about nine brothers and sisters.

Although Martin was born in the town of Eisleben, he really grew up in Mansfeld. Here he had his earliest schooling in the local trivial school. This was a Latin school emphasizing three subjects, grammar, logic, and rhetoric, hence the term *trivial,* from the Latin *trivium.* Martin disliked this school as well as the other two schools where he spent his childhood years.

At fourteen, Martin left home to attend school in Magdeburg. A semimonastic lay order known as the Brethren of the Common Life ran the school. They emphasized a simple practice of Christianity and the importance of the Bible, themes later prominent in Martin's own thinking. But he only stayed at Magdeburg for one year. At fifteen years of age, he moved to Eisenach to study at Saint George's Latin School. Martin sang in the choir and, according to tradition, a young wife named

Ursula Cotta was so taken with his singing that she brought him home. Luther considered his years in Eisenach as among his happiest.

Hans wanted his son to study for the law and so, at seventeen, Martin matriculated at the university of the great city of Erfurt. He first studied philosophy and won his baccalaureate and master of arts degrees. In 1505, he finally began to read the law. However, Martin never wanted to be a lawyer. This intensely religious young man who lived with a great fear of God's wrath and of eternal punishment in hell decided to defy his father's will (as he would one day defy the pope and the emperor) and dedicate his life to serving God as a monk.

Brother Martin, Augustinian

Martin chose one of the strictest of the eleven monasteries in Erfurt at this time: the Reformed Congregation of the Eremetical Order of Saint Augustine. Often wealthy and powerful places, many monasteries had also become quite lax in their performance of the monastic rule. Some houses resisted this slide into easygoing Christianity and were known as reformed or observant houses. Martin joined a strict house, a mendicant monastery, meaning that the brothers lived in community but were expected to beg to support themselves. Many of the Augustinians taught classes at the University of Erfurt. The theology of Saint Augustine formed the backbone of the curriculum, and this would become an important source for Luther's own theological ideas.

Most of the friars were priests, so because of his obvious talents, Brother Martin could expect to be ordained. However, despite Martin's earnest attitude and careful behavior, he approached ordination filled with fear. He faltered at his first mass, with his parents, friends, and monastic colleagues looking on. Sometime later, he declared: "I was utterly stupefied and terror-stricken. . . . 'Shall I, a miserable little pygmy, say, "I want this, I ask for that"? For I am dust and ashes and full of sin and I am speaking to the living, eternal and the true God'" (Bainton, p. 30). His dread was not just a matter of nerves, but signaled a deep unrest, a profound fear that he was not good enough and never could be.

Martin continued his studies. His terror of God continued. Despite long fasts, vigils, prayers, strict observance of the Rule, and frequent confessions, Martin's sense of his unworthiness drove him into profound gloom.

His superior and spiritual director (the German term in use then was *seelsorger*, literally the person who worries about your soul), Johann von Staupitz, decided to treat this unrest by sending Martin deep into the study of Scripture. Of course, Luther knew the basic Bible stories, and he knew the psalms by heart, after all the monks spent large portions of their day chanting the psalms. Otherwise, Martin really knew little about the book. He said of those early studies, "When I read in it, my heart bled." This book would change Martin's whole understanding of church and religion.

Dr. Luther in Wittenberg

Duke Frederick the Wise, who ruled Saxony, wanted the University of Wittenberg to rival that of Leipzig. So he sought to add Augustinian and Franciscan friars to its faculty. Martin's superiors transferred him from Erfurt to Wittenberg. Luther's *seelsorger*, Dr. Staupitz, was dean of the school of theology at the university and began grooming Martin for a larger role in the intellectual life of the Augustinian order, the university, and the church.

Besides the regular monastic duties of prayer, Martin's work schedule kept him intensely busy during these years in Wittenberg. He taught a heavy load of classes while studying for his doctorate in theology. He preached to the monastic chapter and at Saint Mary's parish church. The order elevated him to the position of district vicar with oversight for eleven monasteries. In the midst of his hectic life, some of Martin's energies were still consumed by the doubts that nagged him about the way Christ's church was being run.

In November of 1510, the Augustinians sent Martin to Rome to lay a petition before the pope. This was the longest trip Martin would ever take, and it proved to be an eye-opener.

Martin may have had problems with corruption in the German church, but the Germans, he reported, were earnest about their religion compared with what he found in "Holy Rome." The frivolous and hasty way that Roman priests performed the mass horrified him. He observed that some Roman priests could say six masses in the time it took him to say one (the rule was that a mass must not be completed in less than twelve minutes). When he offered mass at a holy site, waiting priests shouted, *"Passa, passa,"* "get a move on." Even so, Luther the faithful Roman Catholic refused to see this as symptomatic. He did the prescribed pilgrimage tour of holy places to earn indulgences, still hoping to allay his dreadful fears about the unworthiness of his soul. Nevertheless, Martin began to wonder whether all this was really true. Did God really want this kind of worship, this kind of dread?

Stirrings of Reform

After returning from Rome, Martin's superiors permanently assigned him to Wittenberg, and he began in earnest to question and reformulate medieval theology. Under the influence of his biblical study, Martin placed new emphasis on humility as a central Christian virtue. He defined humility as living in total dependence upon God, without presuming to change God through our good works. His reading in the German mystics, especially John Tauler and a compendium that Luther himself republished with a new preface and notes, *A German Theology,* confirmed Martin in his new direction.

Martin turned his criticism toward the institution of monasticism. He observed that too much emphasis was placed on external observances like fasting and strict adherence to rules and not enough on simple Christian virtues like loving one's neighbor.

Next, Luther attacked the Scholastics for replacing the Bible with Aristotle's complicated logic and philosophy. This ignited an academic war at Wittenberg University in which Martin tried, with success, to supplant courses on scholasticism with teaching centered around Scripture, the theology of

Saint Augustine, and the teachings of the early fathers of the church.

Then in the midst of all this tumult, Martin had his transformative tower experience. Luther had his study up in the tower of the Augustinian monastery at Wittenberg. He was reading the Book of Romans where Paul treats the concept of the righteousness of God. Martin had always hated these passages because he saw them as the source of the distance between God and humanity: God is righteous, humans are sinful; God is wrathful and judges us harshly. Now, studying Romans 1:17 ("For in it the righteousness of God is revealed through faith for faith; as it is written, 'The one who is righteous will live by faith'"), a powerful light went on for Martin. Paul's words had little to do with God's judgment, but rather spoke eloquently of God's grace:

> My situation was that, although an impeccable monk, I stood before God as a sinner troubled in conscience, and I had no confidence that my merit would assuage him. Therefore I did not love a just and angry God, but rather hated and murmured against him. Yet I clung to the dear Paul and had a great yearning to know what he meant.
>   . . . Then I grasped that the justice of God is that righteousness by which through grace and sheer mercy God justifies us through faith. Thereupon I felt myself to be reborn and to have gone through open doors into paradise. . . .
>   If you have a true faith that Christ is your Saviour, then at once you have a gracious God, for faith leads you in and opens up God's heart and will, that you should see pure grace and overflowing love. (Bainton, pp. 49–50)

Martin had never heard what these words from Romans were really saying because his indoctrination told him that he had to work his way to perfection. Now he knew that a merciful God had already justified him. His hate of God and fears for his salvation dissipated.

Reformation

The revelation that we are justified by faith through grace alone provided the foundation for Luther's actions during the rest of his life. The tinder that caused this insight to burst into flame was lit by Pope Leo X's Jubilee Indulgence of 1513, which did not find its way to Martin's part of the world until 1517.

The church provided indulgences for dealing with the consequences of our sinfulness. Even Martin understood little about the complicated reasoning behind indulgences until his new theology came into conflict with Leo's indulgence campaign to help build Saint Peter's Basilica. Theologians, then and now, debated exactly what indulgences accomplished and how.

For several centuries, the church had imposed public penance on those who wished forgiveness for grievous or mortal sins. The purpose of the public penance was called satisfaction. Public penance was a way of exacting justice, alongside of granting forgiveness, for serious wrongdoing. No one liked the humiliation involved in public penance, so the idea arose that perhaps people could avoid it if they instead said a series of prayers or made a donation of alms. Monetary restitution became one of the sacrifices or penances that were possible. *Indulgence* literally means "a kindness." Offering indulgences seemed a kindness compared with requiring public penance, especially when the penance might be a pilgrimage to the Holy Land or fasting and praying dressed in sackcloth on the steps of the cathedral.

Combining religious practice and monetary offerings proved dangerous. Someone inevitably asked, "How can we expand this practice and make even more money?" Over the ensuing centuries, the practice of indulgences spread. Soon penitents thought that they could buy their way out of not only public penance but also purgatory, the purifying fire needed to cleanse imperfect souls before the last judgment.

Also, at this time, the concept of the treasury of merit arose. Treasury of merit meant that Jesus and the saints achieved more good works than they needed for their own salvation, and these surplus "merits" could be used by other people through the purchase of indulgences. One could even buy these merits for others, for example, one's dead relatives. The Council of Trent would later denounce these beliefs about buying one's way out of penance or purgatory.

When an indulgence seller like Dominican preacher John Tetzel came to town, he would begin the campaign with a procession, banners waving, flutes and drums playing, and a huge crucifix and the pope's coat of arms being carried before it. When a crowd gathered, the indulgence preacher knew how to talk to his audience, and the indulgence offered by Leo X proved irresistible to many. This jingle summarized the appeal of indulgences to the simple folk listening:

> As soon as the coin in the coffer rings,
> At once the soul up to heaven springs.

Indeed, the practice of indulgences culminated in Leo's Jubilee Indulgence. Historian Roland Bainton describes this indulgence:

> The instructions declared that a plenary indulgence had been issued by His Holiness Pope Leo X to defray the expenses of remedying the sad state of the blessed apostles Peter and Paul and the innumerable martyrs and saints whose bones lay moldering, subject to constant desecration from rain and hail. Subscribers would enjoy a plenary and perfect remission of all sins. They would be restored to the state of innocence which they enjoyed in baptism and would be relieved of all the pains of purgatory, including those incurred by an offense to the Divine Majesty. Those securing indulgences on behalf of the dead already in purgatory need not themselves be contrite and confess their sins. (P. 58)

Father Martin Luther, Augustinian monk, doctor of theology, and parish preacher, was suddenly confronted, not in theory, but in flamboyant practice, with something that called into question everything he was discovering about the "new God" revealed in Jesus.

At this point, Martin did not call for a rejection of indulgences. Instead, he sent an invitation to a disputation, his Ninety-five Theses, to Archbishop Albert of Mainz. Eventually he nailed a copy to the door of the Castle Church in Wittenberg, the university bulletin board where academic disputations were routinely announced. Inviting public discussion of issues was common, especially in university towns. Martin was calling for a public, theological "thinking through" of a practice that he found troubling. The Ninety-five Theses were intended to serve as points for deliberation and debate. The theses were published in Latin for scholars and only later translated into German and circulated widely. Later, Luther would not only reject indulgences but see them as symptomatic of a religious system that had lost its moorings in a fundamental way. But not now.

Open Conflict

Rather than dealing directly with the theses in Germany, Archbishop Albert sent a copy of Martin's theses about the reform of indulgences to Rome. The pope responded by asking the general of the Augustinian order to quietly subdue this unruly monk. At the general chapter of his order, Martin defended his position. This became known as the Heidelberg Disputation. Martin powerfully asserted that his position adhered to that of his order's patron, Saint Augustine. He also, for the first time, began to expound his "theology of the cross." By and large, his brother monks were supportive, even enthusiastic.

Among the Dominican order, Luther's ideas found neither support or enthusiasm. Through their brother Friar John Tetzel, the Dominicans were involved in the campaign to sell the Jubilee Indulgence. The pope asked the Dominicans to press the case against Luther. They charged Friar Sylvester Prierias with responding to Brother Martin's complaints. Accusations of heresy were soon leveled against Martin and forwarded to Rome.

For his part, Martin wrote directly to Pope Leo X, seeking to reassure the pontiff about his orthodoxy and loyalty. Nevertheless, powers around the pope convinced him that Luther had to be suppressed. He was summoned to Rome. His prince, Frederick, quietly refused to send Luther into harm's way and demanded a hearing on German soil. So in October of 1518, Luther traveled to Augsburg to meet with Cardinal Cajetan, one of the pope's ablest theologians.

Cajetan had been instructed to refuse discussion with Brother Martin, to secure his submission and recantation or have him arrested. Martin, however, was not about to consent to such a procedure. He demanded a hearing at which his opinions would be rebutted from Scripture. He and Cajetan sparred for three days, after which the cardinal declined to see him again. After this encounter, John von Staupitz dispensed Martin from his vows as an Augustinian, in effect, releasing him from the community. Martin never lost his respect for and friendship with Dr. Staupitz and the Augustinian tradition, but Martin was going down a road where his mentor could not follow.

The third major event of these years was the debate at Leipzig with Dr. John Eck. Martin and John argued about the power of the pope in the church and thus, inevitably, about the definition of the church itself. This debate, coming on top of Heidelberg and Augsburg, forced Martin to recognize that he differed from the leadership of the church and was advocating thoroughgoing reform of both doctrine and decision-making authority. Motivated by the debates, Luther picked up his pen and wrote three of his most important books—manifestos that would call for renewal of the existing church down to its very roots.

Outlining the Reforms

In Martin's *Address to the Christian Nobility of the German Nation,* he outlined his program of reform for the rulers of his country. Luther called for an end to civil rule by the church. He expressed his belief in the equality of lay and clergy before God and called for a complete overhaul of the church, including a revamping of the papacy that should return to apostolic simplicity, the marriage of priests, the reform of universities (this was more of Martin's campaign to purge Scholasticism from universities), public schools for boys and girls, reduction of the church's income, reduction of the number of festivals and pilgrimages, and an end to persecution of heretics. He de-

clared that "heretics should be vanquished with books, not with burnings" (Bainton, p. 120).

In the long run, one of the most important aspects of the tract is that it was addressed to the secular rulers of Germany. This would eventually lead to the institution known as the state church, which would significantly hobble the Lutheran church throughout northern Europe, just as it hobbled the Catholic church in southern Europe.

The second important book was Martin's *On the Babylonian Captivity of the Church*. Here Martin called into question the sacramental system of the medieval church. Luther reinterpreted the definition of sacraments, shifting from seven to three: Baptism, Eucharist, and Penance (in other writings, Luther combined Penance under Baptism, but in this book he listed it as a sacrament). In any case, what was most important was how Martin restated the meaning of these sacraments. He believed that the medieval church had turned the sacraments into acts done by the church Godward. Martin took special aim at the notion that the Mass is a sacrifice performed by the church before God. For Luther, the real importance of the sacraments was in what God is doing before us, in us, for us. The sacraments are means of grace; they are the real presence of God interrupting our lives and restoring creation. Because of the emphasis on the power of the priest, simple people had come to view the Mass as a form of magic. Martin emphasized God's loving self-gift to us, God's action, not ours.

The third important work, and still the most approachable, was *The Freedom of the Christian*, a work dedicated to the pope. In this book, Luther tried to explain his concept of faith and of the results of faith. Christian life arises naturally out of faith. Believers no longer do good works to earn something; they do them because they are a new people living out of forgiveness. Christians' love of God motivates them to turn naturally to their neighbors and their need, not out of duty, but out of joy. Church should not be about burdensome rules and regulations, but rather about finally being free to be a real human.

Bellum

While Martin wrote furiously in Germany, in May 1520, the pope published his decree, or bull, *Exsurge Domine (Arise, O Lord)*, condemning Luther as a heretic. This formalized the breach. Martin wrote, "Luther, who is used to *bellum* [war], is not afraid of *bullam*" (Bainton, p. 125). On 10 December 1520, he publicly burned the papal bull outside the Elster gate at Wittenberg. In other towns in Germany and Italy, mobs burned Luther's works. The war was on.

At the beginning of 1521, the pope completed the process of Luther's excommunication in the bull *Decet Romanum*. He also sent Jerome Aleander to Germany to secure the government's support. The young emperor, Charles V, and the imperial parliament, or diet, met in the city of Worms to decide Luther's fate. According to European law, a secular ruler had to arrest and punish heretics, which usually meant burning them at the stake. Aleander pushed for Martin's legal proscription. Luther came to Worms to defend himself. This was probably the most dramatic moment of Martin's dramatic life. Martin would not yield; neither would his opponents.

Finally, the emperor declared Martin to be an outlaw. Even so, Frederick the Wise refused to enforce the ban in Saxony. To protect Martin, Frederick staged his kidnapping. Over the next months, safe in the castle at Wartburg, Martin translated the Bible from Latin into German. Eventually, he returned to Wittenberg. Martin could not leave his home country, but he was free to write from it and direct others in the burgeoning Reformation Movement.

The Church Is Divided

The process of actually making specific changes in the theology and practice of Christianity now began to be implemented in territories supportive of Martin's ideas. It did not happen overnight. The Lutheran movement continued to see itself as within the traditional catholic structure at least up until the Diet of Augsburg in 1530, and even after that there was a clear intention to renew, not divide, the church. Those who accepted Martin's ideas were uncertain as to how to view themselves.

Nevertheless, three main lines of reform took shape:

The Bible: The Holy Scriptures were given a new weight. The Bible went from being a liturgical book and a theologian's book, to being the people's book and the central authority in the church's teaching.

The liturgy: Martin pruned away some of the more extravagant ceremonies, especially Corpus Christi, the veneration of countless saints, and inappropriate devotion to the Blessed Virgin. His most radical reform was his extensive eucharistic renewal, much of which is the common practice of Catholics and Protestants today.

Luther kept statues, windows, traditional music and vesture, altars, and the basic faith and rituals of the Mass. He did translate the Mass into the vernacular, but ironically, this reform is misunderstood. Luther wrote two Mass forms, one in Latin and one in German. He conceived the Latin form to be the standard one; the German one was for rural parishes where no one knew Latin. Latin remained the main liturgical language for Lutherans long after Martin's death. Reflecting the primacy of God's word, he did insist on the sermon, the lessons, and many hymns being in German. Martin was a prolific and talented hymnist, and many of his hymns are still sung today. His liturgical reforms were much less dramatic than those made by the Catholic church at Vatican Council II.

The hierarchy: Martin did not want to do away with bishops. For instance, in Scandinavia where the kings engineered a total implementation of the Reformation from the top down, the episcopal office was maintained virtually intact. To this day, pastors are still addressed as priests. However, Martin did want to reform the hierarchy.

First, he wanted to take "the sword" out of the bishop's hands. Worldly rule was to be prohibited to bishops. Second, the magisterium, or teaching office, was to be strictly subordinate to Scripture. For example, it was amenable to Martin for a bishop to proclaim a fast, but it was not permissible to make the fast mandatory and failure to comply a sin against God. Third, Martin believed that the bishops should be primarily pastors. Their real job was to preach and teach the Gospel and to ensure that clergy under their supervision did the same.

Settling Down

After the dramatic events of Martin's early life, matters settled down into the less exciting task of consolidation and the creation of institutions for those "Catholics in exile" who felt constrained to follow in Martin's new way.

Like many of his followers who had been priests or monks, Luther married. He and Katherine began their family. Martin was a devoted husband and father, an active pastor, a busy teacher, and a prolific writer. For example, his lectures just on Genesis take up eight volumes. He became dean of the university, and, of course, he supervised the introduction of the Reformation at home and abroad.

Alongside all this productive work, however, another side of Martin's personality began to emerge more and more often. Martin had always been a vigorous and polemical fighter in a very polemical age. He could be devastating in his attacks on his opponents, but in his later years, he seems to have gone overboard. He pictured any opponents as coarse and brutal demons. He wrote horrifying, scatological books against the Catholic church, the non-Lutheran Protestant church, the Turks, and most disturbing of all in the light of its consequences, the Jews. He called for the burning of synagogues; the denial of property, education, and basic civil rights to Jews; and the forced deportation of Jews.

Some ascribe his excesses to ill health and old age, and he did suffer terrible afflictions. Some blame his excesses on a fanatical belief in the power of the devil, although Luther's views on this subject were standard for his age. Some cite political pressures, especially after the formation of the League of Smalkalden in 1531 transformed the Lutheran movement into a political and military alliance. In any case, his increasing irascibility ultimately remains a mystery.

For the last decades of his life, Martin devoted himself to the gracious God he had encountered in the tower years before. He died as he lived, undeterred by obstacles, filled with faith. In 1545, a request came to him to settle a feud between the counts of Mansfeld. His physician and others warned that he would never survive such a trip in the depths of winter. Martin completed the journey to Eisleben, settled the argument, preached, and counseled. Worn out, he suffered a series of heart attacks and died in the city of his birth, the very year that the Catholic bishops gathered for the Council of Trent to begin the Catholic Reformation.

The Spirituality of Martin Luther

Grace alone: For Martin, Christian spirituality has its source in God, is sustained by the grace of God, and finds its goal in God. Without grace, the human subject remains essentially passive, even unwilling. Spirituality is not a movement of the soul, but something that happens to the soul. It is not about our aspiration for God, since in Martin's view we don't aspire to God.

Christ alone: Salvation comes through the life, death, and Resurrection of Christ alone. For Martin, the old Adam, our vaunted self, needs to die on the cross. Then in the resurrection moment, our real self, which is found in Christ, can awaken. It has been locked in sleep like Brunhilda in her ring of fire on a remote mountaintop. Now, out of the ashes of the old Adam, Christ breaks through and awakens his bride. The new world of agape, selfless love, joy, and peace, has broken in through Christ alone.

The Word: Therefore, if we want to find God, we do not start by looking inward to the ego. We start with the Word that only God speaks, the Word made flesh in Jesus. God continues to speak this Word in the community called church, gathered around Scripture, sermon, and sacrament. Prayer should begin here as well.

Prayer: When Martin's barber, Peter Beskendorf, asked his pastor to teach him to pray, Luther told him to pray the catechism: that is, the Ten Commandments, the Lord's Prayer, the Apostles' Creed. He encouraged him to meditate on each commandment, petition, and article. At a minimum, said Martin, at rising each morning and upon retiring each evening, time should be set aside for God. Martin suggested this order for prayer at morning and evening:

How the head of the family shall teach his household to say morning and evening prayers

In the morning, when you rise, make the sign of the cross and say, "In the name of God, the Father, the Son, and the Holy Spirit. Amen."

Then, kneeling or standing, say the Apostles' Creed and the Lord's Prayer. Then you may say this prayer:

"I give Thee thanks, heavenly Father, through thy dear Son Jesus Christ, that Thou hast protected me through the night from all harm and danger. I beseech Thee to keep me this day, too, from all sin and evil, that in all my thoughts, words, and deeds I may please Thee. Into thy hands I commend my body and soul and all that is mine. Let thy holy angels have charge of me, that the wicked one may have no power over me. Amen."

After singing a hymn (possibly a hymn on the Ten Commandments) or whatever your devotion may suggest, you should go to your work joyfully.

In the evening, when you retire, make the sign of the cross and say, "In the name of God, the Father, the Son, and the Holy Spirit. Amen."

Then, kneeling or standing, say the Apostles' Creed and the Lord's Prayer. Then you may say this prayer:

"I give Thee thanks, heavenly Father, through thy dear Son Jesus Christ, that Thou hast this day graciously protected me. I beseech Thee to forgive all my sin and the wrong which I have done. Graciously protect me during the coming night. Into thy hands I commend my body and soul and all that is mine. Let thy holy angels have charge of me, that the wicked one may have no power over me. Amen."

Then quickly lie down and sleep in peace. (Tappert, pp. 352–353)

The priesthood of all believers: Martin taught that the church is a great priesthood. Every baptized Christian has a priestly ministry to exercise in prayer, faith, and Christian living in the vocation to which God has called each one. Ordained men and women are called to restore the laity to their full partnership with the ordained in the work of Christ. Every baptized person is part of Christ's address to the world.

Martin Luther Today

Martin witnesses in a timeless way that the Word of God is life. He urges us to have absolute confidence in God, who sent us Jesus, the light of the world, and who pours out the grace that sets us free. Martin called the church, the People of God, to constant renewal by listening to the word of God. Martin teaches us to be people of prayer, inviting the Holy Spirit to enliven us with the truth of the Scriptures. In a world divided by so many factions and ideologies, Martin reminds us to be ruled by faith in the Gospel and guided by love.

Finally, as Cardinal Willebrands remarked, "In this we could all learn from him that God must always remain the Lord, and that our most important human answer must always remain absolute confidence in God" (Rusch and Gros, p. 13).

✧ Meditation 1 ✧

Dread

Theme: Martin Luther's faith and spirituality begin not with the experience of God's presence but with the terrifying experience of God's absence. Luther called this the experience of the hidden God who seems not to care and is even filled with wrath.

Opening prayer: Dear God, give me courage when my life is dark and you seem far away.

About Martin

Martin Luther grew up in a church that portrayed God and even Jesus as angry judges of our terrible human weaknesses. He became an Augustinian friar hoping to allay the wrath of God by living a perfect life, but he could not seem to get past an overwhelming fear of God. He once kept his confessor in the confessional for six hours as he tried to purify his sick soul. But God remained hidden and silent.

In 1507, Luther was ordained a priest and said his first Mass. This moment stayed with him for the rest of his life. It should have been a time of great joy for the young monk, but instead Luther was filled with a terrible sense of being lost. Luther recounts his thoughts when he came to the words of the mass, "We offer unto thee, the living, the true, the eternal God":

> At these words I was utterly stupefied and terror stricken. I thought to myself, "With what tongue shall I address such Majesty, seeing that all men ought to tremble in the presence of even an earthly prince? Who am I, that I should lift up mine eyes or raise my hands to the divine Majesty? The angels surround him. At his nod the earth trembles. And shall I, a miserable little pygmy, say 'I want this, I ask for that'? For I am dust and ashes and full of sin and I am speaking to the living, eternal and the true God." (Bainton, p. 30)

Many of the world-changing events that Luther would precipitate in the years to come would spring from his efforts to solve the problem of the hidden God. He opened a door for millions of tormented souls. But he also understood that every person must face the experience of God's overwhelming silence. Until people descend into this kind of hell, they cannot reach heaven.

Pause: Can you be honest with God and with yourself about those dark places and times when loneliness, fear, and guilt overwhelm you?

Martin's Words

Luther's God was the Almighty One of the Bible. God was the creator of "weal and woe," in Isaiah's terms, and all persons must face their life and death before the face of this God:

> Therefore it is a profound saying when Moses prays: "Thou causest men to die." He is saying: "It is Thy work; because of Thy wrath the entire race is swallowed up by death." Men do not come into being by accident. They are not born by accident. They do not suffer by accident. They do not die by accident. Even animals do not die by accident. They die because we make them die (Gen. 1:28). Their experiences are directed by man. How much more

is death and the end of man's life due to a definite cause! Therefore as life is the result of God's designing, so death is the result of God's wrath. It is He who causes man to die. It is He who plunges him from life into death. (Pelikan, *Luther's Works*, vol. 13, pp. 96–97)

This hidden and wrathful God threw Brother Martin into fear and despair. Only much later would Luther understand the purpose of God's hiddenness and the purpose of our despair:

It is obviously . . . utterly repugnant to common sense, for God to be guided only by His own will when He abandons man, hardens his heart, and damns him. For He seems to take pleasure in the sins and in the eternal torment of the unfortunate ones, even though preachers praise the greatness of His mercy and loving-kindness. It seems that for this reason one must look upon God as unfair and brutal, as unbearable. This repugnant thought has caused many distinguished people of all times to go to pieces. And who would not find it repugnant? More than once it hurled me down into the deepest abyss of despair and made me wish I had never been born—until I learned how salutary this despair is and how close it is to grace. (Elert, p. 22)

Reflection

Martin Luther asks us to begin our spiritual journey in a hard place. His nineteenth-century follower, Søren Kierkegaard, was saying something similar when he said that Christianity begins with our confronting the night-fear that life might be absurd and meaningless. His twentieth-century follower, Paul Tillich, believed that the Christian journey begins precisely when we face our estrangement from God.

For Luther, one of the most important moments in the New Testament was when Christ, nailed to the cross, cried out, "My God, my God, why have you forsaken me?" This was proof to Luther that the Incarnation was the real thing.

Jesus shares our human lot right to the bone—our feeling of abandonment by God.

Luther had spent his whole youth trying to meet the absolute demands of a righteous God, but he was unable. He was unable to meet even the lesser demands of his own conscience. Luther often said that the law of God is a mirror that shows us who we really are. But every time he looked in that mirror, he saw a sad tale of failure. He saw a sinner. God was asking—demanding—that Luther be someone other than who he was, than who he would ever be capable of being. He felt utterly cut off from God, from life, from hope. Eventually, Luther came to realize, as he said, that this despair was actually close to grace.

✧ When have you felt utterly cut off from God, from life, from hope? When have you cried out, "My God, my God, why have you forsaken me?" Recall and be with these times.

✧ Ponder your feelings about lamentation as authentic prayer. Read Psalm 22 or 88, and then ask yourself:
✦ Do I have the courage of the psalmists who bitterly complained to God?
✦ Is our prayer life an escape from the dark and terrifying aspects of human life or a place where we can dare to face all of our life before God?

✧ Write a letter to God, as you might to a parent or mentor, and tell God about a time when you felt let down or abandoned.

✧ Ultimately, Luther's argument with God became the impetus for entering more deeply and in new ways into the meaning of God. Luther's fear and even hatred of God became important parts of his journey to the new God revealed in the Gospel. Can you think of ways your struggles with life's pain and sorrow have helped you—perhaps even forced you—to grow into a more mature understanding of and relationship with God?

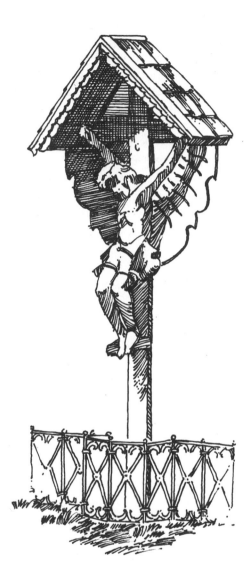

God's Word

I do not understand my own actions. For I do not do
what I want, but I do the very thing I hate. Now if I do
what I do not want, I agree that the law is good. But in
fact it is no longer I that do it, but sin that dwells within

me. For I know that nothing good dwells within me, that is, in my flesh. I can will what is right, but I cannot do it. For I do not do the good I want, but the evil I do not want is what I do. Now if I do what I do not want, it is no longer I that do it, but sin that dwells within me.

So I find it to be a law that when I want to do what is good, evil lies close at hand. For I delight in the law of God in my inmost self, but I see in my members another law at war with the law of my mind, making me captive to the law of sin that dwells in my members. Wretched man that I am! Who will rescue me from this body of death? Thanks be to God through Jesus Christ our Lord! (Romans 7:15–25a)

Closing prayer:

Look, Lord, an empty vessel that needs to be filled. My Lord, fill it. I am weak in the faith; strengthen me. I am cold in love; warm me and make me fervent, that my love may go out to my neighbor. I do not have a strong and firm faith. At times I doubt and am unable to trust you completely. O Lord, help me. Strengthen my faith and trust in you. I have insured all my treasure in your name. I am poor; you are rich and you did come to be merciful to the poor. I am a sinner; you are upright. With me there is an abundance of sin; with you a fullness of righteousness. Therefore I will remain with you, from whom I can receive but to whom I may not give. (Brokering, pp. 67–68)

Christ Alone

Theme: If the great problem facing humankind is the silence of God, the solution to this problem is the Incarnation. In Jesus, God comes out of hiding. Jesus Christ reveals God and God's benevolent will to all people.

Opening prayer: Holy Jesus, open my eyes to see the One whom you call Abba.

About Martin

In the midst of all his painful fears and questions, young Brother Martin was blessed to have a caring and sensitive spiritual director, the vicar of his Augustinian order for that part of Germany, Johann von Staupitz. To Dr. Staupitz, Luther confessed hatred for the hidden, wrathful God who condemned him to despair and death. Staupitz encouraged his young monk to look at God's grace and love in his son, Jesus Christ.

Staupitz decided to treat Martin's malaise by sending him deep into the study of the Holy Scriptures. He ordered Luther to begin biblical studies toward a degree of doctor of theology. He intended for Luther to one day occupy his chair as professor of biblical theology at Wittenberg University. Brother

Martin felt overwhelmed by the task, but he obeyed his beloved mentor and superior.

In 1513, Luther began his lectures on the Book of Psalms at the university. Many of the psalms were profound laments, and in accord with the prevailing interpretation of his times, Luther understood them to refer to Christ, especially Psalm 22, which Jesus cried out from the cross: "My God, my God, why have you forsaken me?" Like his contemporaries, Luther believed that all of the Old Testament pointed forward to Christ, and all of the New Testament was fulfilled in Christ.

A light began to dawn for Martin Luther. He began to see in Jesus Christ a new God: not a hidden, angry, holier-than-thou God, but a God planted deep in the world, deep in human bodies, deep in human lostness. In Jesus, God truly was Emmanuel — God-with-us. In his catechism and in his little guide to prayer written for Master Peter, his barber, Luther emphasized the importance of the biblical pronouns. Why did Jesus suffer and die? *For me.* Not for the sins of an abstract world, but *for my* sins. Jesus, says Martin to his barber, is the Word given to us personally. Jesus smiles on *me* and calls *me* God's child.

In his booklet on prayer for Master Peter, Martin wrote:

Here again a great light shines and teaches us that through Christ, God's Son, we have been redeemed from the death into which we fell after the creation through Adam's sin and otherwise must perish eternally. And this is the time when you remember this. [When you recite the second article of the creed.] Just as you had in the first article to count yourself a creature of God and never doubt it, so here, too, you must count yourself among the redeemed and never doubt it. Of all the words in it you must put first the word "our"; Jesus Christ, *our* Lord, suffered for *us,* died for *us,* rose again for *us,* so that everything is for us and applies to us, and you, too, are included in that "our." So the word is given to us personally. (Doberstein, p. 459)

Pause: Ask yourself: Is Jesus a figure of history, the founder of my religion, or is he more, the incarnate reality of God's love for me?

Martin's Words

In his commentaries on Saint John's Gospel, Luther underscored the centrality of Christ as our way of access to God:

> The body of Christ was God's temple, His castle and palace, His royal hall. We should note this well. So God had bound Himself to the temple at Jerusalem, which is now to end, not indeed for His own sake but for the sake of the people, who, for this reason, had a definite place where they knew they could find God. Therefore He wanted to be nowhere else, and whoever wanted to call upon Him and come before Him had to come to Jerusalem into the Temple or at least turn his face toward it, no matter at what place in the world he might be. For at Jerusalem were the temple and the habitation of God. But now, in the New Testament, God has prepared a different temple in which He wills to dwell. This is the dear humanity of our Lord Jesus Christ. There God desires to let Himself be found, and nowhere else. He calls Christ's body the temple in which God dwells so that all our hearts and eyes may be directed to Christ and we may worship Him alone who sits at the right hand of God in heaven, as we confess in our Christian creed. . . . For Christ is the true Mercy Seat, with whom we find pure grace, pure love, pure friendliness. (Plass, pp. 160–161)

Reflection

The Christ of the Middle Ages had become a somewhat abstract figure: a philosophical Christ, a dogmatic Christ, a divine Christ. But Luther's earthiness and love of life required a truly and fully incarnate God. Martin embraced the humanity of Christ in Jesus of Nazareth, not merely his historical humanity, but a humanity that was still really present for ordinary folk in the toil and trouble of their ordinary lives.

Luther had been taught to think of God as impassable, beyond all suffering and pain, an all-powerful and all-knowing God wrapped in eternal glory. But in Jesus, Luther found another God, a God who is located in the midst of all our suffering and heartache, a God who cares, who weeps, who yearns, who loves. Brother Martin found that his search for God led to a dead end of speculation, or worse, to the hiddenness of God. But then, in a wonderful moment of pure grace, Martin realized that he did not need to find God because in Jesus, God had found him! In encountering Jesus of Nazareth, he was grasped by an eternal love.

✧ Reread "Martin's Words" slowly and meditatively. If a particular line or phrase seems to hold special import, stay with it, letting its meaning for you become clearer.

✧ One of Martin's favorite sayings was *Christus pro me,* "Christ for me." Sitting upright in a comfortable position, repeat this phrase slowly and prayerfully. As any feelings or images come to mind, note them, then let them go, and continue repeating the prayer.

✧ Luther advocated using the crucifix as an object for meditation on the sufferings of Christ for the love of the world. This should not be a time to think about theories of atonement or other theological issues, but rather to be with Jesus as he is suffering for us. Find a crucifix and do likewise.

✧ Meditate on these questions: In what times or places has Jesus seemed most real to me? Can I remember particular instances when I felt especially close to Jesus?

✧ Ask yourself: Am I open to the presence of Christ for me? If I am reluctant or ambivalent, what are the obstacles? Are there ways I am afraid to turn my life over to Christ?

God's Word

"Do not let your hearts be troubled. Believe in God, believe also in me. In my Father's house there are many dwelling places. If it were not so, would I have told you that I go to prepare a place for you? And if I go and prepare a place for you, I will come again and will take you to myself, so that where I am, there you may be also. And you know the way to the place where I am going." Thomas said to him, "Lord, we do not know where you are going. How can we know the way?" Jesus said to him, "I am the way, and the truth, and the life. No one comes to the Father except through me. If you know me, you will know my Father also. From now on you do know him and have seen him."

Philip said to him, "Lord, show us the Father, and we will be satisfied." Jesus said to him, "Have I been with you all this time, Philip, and you still do not know me? Whoever has seen me has seen the Father. How can you say, 'Show us the Father'? Do you not believe that I am in the Father and the Father is in me? The words that I say to you I do not speak on my own; but the Father who dwells in me does his works. Believe me that I am in the Father and the Father is in me; but if you do not, then believe me because of the works themselves." (John 14:1–11)

Closing prayer:

O dearest Jesus, holy child,
Prepare a bed, soft, undefiled,
A holy shrine, within my heart,
That you and I need never part.

(Luther, "From Heaven Above")

✧ Meditation 3 ✧

Grace Alone

Theme: <u>If when Luther looked at God without Christ</u> he <u>saw only silence and wrath,</u> when he looked at himself without Christ, he saw only guilt and sin. This led Martin to the central assertion of his reform movement: Human beings are saved by God's grace alone.

Opening prayer: Dear God, help me to the place of real freedom. Help me to know that all I am, all I do, all I will be, is a gift.

About Martin

Guides at the Wartburg Castle in the Thuringian forest often show visitors the room that they claim was Martin Luther's during his ten-month exile from Wittenburg following the Diet of Worms. They may even point to a discolored spot on the wall where, according to legend, Martin threw an inkpot at the devil.

Many historians dismiss this tale, but it could have happened. It was completely in character for Martin, who once said, "<u>The Devil is moored to me with mighty cords</u>" (Brown, p. 227). For Luther, the devil was not a metaphor or a bad influence on our lives, rather the devil was the lord and ruler of this world, and we are all the devil's slaves. Our wills are in bondage to sin and Satan.

This belief led to one of Martin's most controversial, but also most basic, beliefs: he denied that there is any such thing as free will before God's grace. We might be able to choose what we eat, but we cannot choose the right moral or spiritual course for our life because before God's grace we are in bondage to sin. The men and women of the Renaissance found Luther's denial of free will to be deeply offensive. Holding to this belief, Luther parted company with another great sixteenth-century reformer, the humanist Erasmus of Rotterdam. Erasmus declared this parting of ways with his book *On the Freedom of the Will*. Luther read Erasmus with great interest and said, "You alone have gone to the heart of the problem instead of debating the papacy, indulgences, purgatory, and similar trifles. You alone have gone to the core, and I thank you for it" (Bainton, p. 196).

In response to Erasmus, Luther wrote *The Bondage of the Will* in 1525. In the book, Luther addresses each argument to Erasmus directly:

> You [Erasmus] describe the power of 'free-will' as small, as wholly ineffective apart from the grace of God. Agreed? Now then, I ask you: if God's grace is wanting, if it is taken away from that small power, what can it do? It is ineffective, you say, and can do nothing good. So it will not do what God or His grace wills. Why? Because we have now taken God's grace away from it, and what the grace of God does not do is not good. Hence it follows that 'free-will' without God's grace is not free at all, but is the permanent prisoner and bondslave of evil, since it cannot turn itself to good. . . . Note, however, that if we meant by 'the power of free-will' the power which makes human beings fit subjects to be caught up by the Spirit and touched by God's grace, as creatures made for eternal life or eternal death, we should have a proper definition. . . .
>
> It is a settled truth, then, even on the basis of your own testimony, that we do everything of necessity, and nothing by 'free-will'; for the power of 'free-will' is nil,

and it does no good, nor can do, without grace. (Dillenberger, pp. 187–188)

For Luther, freedom of the will is the great delusion. The actual content of the Fall is the lie, "I can be or do something on my own without God." Freedom is not to be found in the human will, but in the grace of God. The good news is that God does not stop loving humanity because of defective wills, because it is entangled in the devil's web of sinfulness. Humans are like the prodigal son, whose repentance is self-serving, but even so God embraces him and humanity nonetheless. The embrace of grace alone saves and frees.

Pause: Do you see yourself as you are or as you would like to be?

Martin's Words

I frankly confess that, for myself, even if it could be, I should not want "free-will" to be given me, nor anything to be left in my own hands to enable me to endeavour after salvation; not merely because in face of so many dangers, and adversities, and assaults of devils, I could not stand my ground and hold fast my "free-will" (for one devil is stronger than all men, and on these terms no man could be saved); but because, even were there no dangers, adversities, or devils, I should still be forced to labor with no guarantee of success, and to beat my fists at the air. If I lived and worked to all eternity, my conscience would never reach comfortable certainty as to how much it must do to satisfy God. Whatever work I had done, there would still be a nagging doubt as to whether it pleased God, or whether He required something more. The experience of all who seek righteousness by works proves that; and I learned it well enough myself over a period of many years, to my own great hurt. But now that God has taken my salvation out of the control of my own will, and put it under the control of His, and promised to save me, not according to my working or running, but according to

His own grace and mercy, I have the comfortable certainty that He is faithful and will not lie to me, and that He is also great and powerful, so that no devils or opposition can break Him or pluck me from Him. "No one," He says, "shall pluck them out of my hand, because my Father which gave them me is greater than all" (John 10:28–29). Thus it is that, if not all, yet some, indeed many, are saved; whereas, by the power of "free-will" none at all could be saved, but everyone of us would perish. (Dillenberger, p. 199)

Reflection

For Luther, the doctrine of free will is the content of the Fall because it is a refusal of creatureliness, of finitude. The first parents did not want to be humble, contingent creatures, totally dependent on God for their lives. Even though they had been created "good" in God's image, they wanted to be God, thus knowing good *and* evil.

The alternative was humility, the word coming from the Latin *humus*, meaning to be a creature of the earth and satisfied with this placement. The humble person lives life *coram Deo*, before God.

From Adam and Eve to the present day, trouble arises from our unwillingness to live in the freedom that comes from embracing God's will. Instead, we want our own will. One permanent result is war: my free willing and someone else's free willing collide. Jesus, in debate with the Pharisees, said: "Listen to me, all of you, and understand: there is nothing outside a person that by going in can defile, but the things that come out are what defile. . . . For it is from within, from the human heart, that evil intentions come" (Mark 7:14–15, 21). In other words, Jesus tells the Pharisees and us that the problem is corrupt wills.

The solution comes from God. (It does not come from our abdicating free will and returning to God's will. We are not capable of doing that because we don't have a free will.) The Good News is grace: that is, God does not stop loving us, refuses to stop loving us, will never stop loving us. We will be saved, our life will be salvaged because the one free Being in the universe will settle for nothing less. Only God's grace can save us, not our willing.

✧ Pray the first half of the Lord's Prayer several times, pausing between each repetition for meditation:

Our Father in Heaven, hallowed be *your* name.
your kingdom come, *your will be done,*
on earth (in my life) as in Heaven.

✧ Ponder again these words of Luther: "If we meant by 'the power of free-will' the power which makes human beings fit subjects to be caught up by the Spirit and touched by God's grace, as creatures made for eternal life or eternal death, we should have a proper definition." How do you feel about this understanding of the power of free will? Share your feelings with God.

✧ Read the parable of the prodigal and his brother in Luke 15:11–32. Are either the sinner (the prodigal) or the righteous one (the elder brother) free? How can they become free?

✧ Luther was not interested in grace as a theological doctrine or as a legal loophole; he was interested in grace as a way of life. Try to imagine, concretely, what a life, your life, would look like if every moment were lived as a gift of God's grace.

✧ One of the most bothersome things about "grace alone" is that it is all or nothing. I cannot say, "I deserve God's grace, but so-and-so doesn't." If grace is deserved, it is not grace. Am I willing to let people I despise be saved too? Think of a totally horrid person like Adolf Hitler or Joseph Stalin. Can you learn to desire his or her salvation?

✧ This would be a good time to sing each verse of "Amazing Grace." Pause between stanzas for silent reflection.

Amazing grace, how sweet the sound,
That saved a wretch like me!
I once was lost, but now am found;
Was blind, but now I see.

'Twas grace that taught my heart to fear,
And grace my fears relieved;
How precious did that grace appear
The hour I first believed!

Through many dangers, toils, and snares
I have already come;
'Tis grace has brought me safe thus far,
And grace will lead me home.

The Lord has promised good to me;
His Word my hope secures;
He will my shield and portion be
As long as life endures.

(Newton, hymn 448)

God's Word

You were dead through the trespasses and sins in which you once lived, following the course of this world, following the ruler of the power of the air, the spirit that is now at work among those who are disobedient. All of us once lived among them in the passions of our flesh, following the desires of flesh and senses, and we were by nature children of wrath, like everyone else. But God, who is rich in mercy, out of the great love with which he loved us even when we were dead through our trespasses, made us alive together with Christ—by grace you have been saved—and raised us up with him and seated us with him in the heavenly places in Christ Jesus, so that in the ages to come he might show the immeasurable riches of his grace in kindness toward us in Christ Jesus. For by grace you have been saved through faith, and this is not your own doing; it is the gift of God—not the result of works, so that no one may boast. For we are what he has made us, created in Christ Jesus for good works, which God prepared beforehand to be our way of life. (Ephesians 2:1–10)

Closing prayer: "O God, Father in heaven, look in mercy upon your needy children, and grant us grace. Amen" (Brokering, p. 18).

✦ Meditation 4 ✦

Faith Alone

Theme: The gift of God's grace in Jesus Christ creates a new way of being in the world, a new way of life. Martin Luther calls this new way of living, faith. Christ is the content of the new life; faith is the means by which we enter into Christ's life for us.

Opening prayer: God of love, open the eyes of our hearts that we may see the world anew.

About Martin

On All Hallow's Eve 1517, Father Martin walked across the main square of the small town of Wittenberg to nail his Ninety-five Theses to the door of the Castle Church. He had previously sent a copy to the primate of Germany, Archbishop Albert of Mainz.

Luther was protesting the preaching of the Jubilee Indulgence proclaimed by Pope Leo X to raise revenue for the building of Saint Peter's Basilica in Rome. In Wittenberg, All Saints' Day included a special viewing of the Castle Church's huge collection of holy relics that numbered 17,433 and included nine thorns from Christ's crown, thirty-five splinters of the true cross, straw from the manger, one piece of Jesus' swaddling cloths, one piece of bread from the Last Supper, one vial of milk from the Blessed Virgin Mary, and so on. Viewing the relics and the promise of indulgences raised a lot of money. But Luther's Ninety-five Theses challenged these practices and offered to participate in debate about the time-honored sale of indulgences. The Reformation was under way.

Luther argued that this practice "made out of God a merchant, who would give the Kingdom of Heaven not freely, out of grace, but for money and human achievement" (Brown, p. 229). He claimed that through indulgences the devil sets up shop in our soul. But indulgences were, for Luther, only the tip of the iceberg. They were a particularly coarse example of a much bigger problem: the common belief that good works bring about human salvation without grace.

Luther was asked: If you take away all human effort, what will you put in its place? His answer was simple: faith. Human beings are saved by God's grace alone through faith. We are saved on account of Christ and through faith.

Pause: Look deep within. Who or what do you ultimately trust to make sense of your life?

Martin's Words

Commenting on Galatians 2:4–5 in 1531, Martin wrote:

> The true Gospel teaches that works and love do not dress or perfect faith, but that faith of itself is the gift of God and the divine work in the heart which justifies because it apprehends Christ the Savior Himself. Human reason looks to the Law: This I have done; this I have not done.— But when faith performs its proper office, it looks to absolutely nothing except Jesus Christ, the Son of God, given for the sins of the whole world. It does not look at love, does not say: What have I done? Which sin have I committed? What have I merited? It rather says: What has Christ done? What has He merited? (Plass, p. 496)

Reflection

We will misunderstand and distort Luther's concept of salvation by faith alone if we confuse faith with belief. Faith does believe, but it is much more than accepting certain propositions about God and Christ as true. Faith is closer to love than it is to belief if by belief we mean assent to certain propositions. For Martin, faith is a living relationship that we each have with God because of our encounter with Jesus of Nazareth. In faith, we do not just believe in Jesus, we take a hold of him. We have him present in our heart and life. Luther, who loved homey images, even went so far as to say that by faith Christ and the Christian are baked into one cake. Faith is the clamp by which hearts are held together and joined with Christ.

Another vital aspect of Luther's doctrine of faith was what Paul Tillich was trying to explain when he equated Luther's concept of faith with ultimate concern. He got this idea from Luther's words in the *Large Catechism:* "A god is that to which we look for all good and in which we find refuge in every time of need. To have a god is nothing else than to trust and believe him with our whole heart" (Tappert, p. 365).

We have many concerns in our life, and we negotiate among those concerns every day as we seek to live in a complex and demanding world. But how do we conduct these negotiations? How do we prioritize? How do we make choices? Sometimes our choices may seem to be completely random and arbitrary, but Luther understood that if we dig deep enough, we will discover a direction, a master issue, an ultimate concern behind our choices. This is our faith, and whether we are conscious of it or not, it is molding our life and our decisions.

Justifying faith is faith that has found its proper object. Indeed, the Lutheran definition of idolatry or false faith is to treat something as ultimate when it really is not. Christian faith is a reorientation of one's whole life to Jesus Christ. Martin Luther teaches that Christian faith has three fundamental aspects:

1. Saving faith is faith in God's grace offered to us in Jesus the Christ.
2. Faith is a living relationship with God through Christ.
3. Faith is about ultimates. To have faith in God means that in the God revealed by Jesus, we find the meaning of our life.

✧ A man came to Jesus with a sick son and asked for healing (Mark 9:14–29). Jesus responded that such healing could only occur through faith. The man then cried out, "I believe; help my unbelief!" Imagine that you are this man, standing before Jesus. Ask yourself: What is my belief? What is my unbelief? What kind of help do I need from Jesus for my unbelief?

✧ Spend some time reading about your own faith: read the debit column of your checkbook or examine all the cards, pictures, and so on in your wallet or purse. What do these things tell you about your priorities? Do they give you a clue to what your ultimate concern might be?

✧ In 1998, both the Vatican and the Lutheran World Federation approved the "Joint Declaration on the Doctrine of Justification." After five hundred years of conflict, Lutherans and Catholics finally recognized their common understanding of this key belief. Meditate on this important passage from the "Joint Declaration:"

> In faith we together [Lutherans and Catholics] hold the conviction that justification is the work of the triune God. The Father sent his Son into the world to save sinners. The foundation and presupposition of justification is the incarnation, death and resurrection of Christ. Justification thus means that Christ himself is our righteousness, in which we share through the Holy Spirit in accord with the will of the Father. Together we confess: By grace alone, in faith in Christ's saving work and not because of any merit on our part, we are accepted by God and receive the Holy Spirit, who renews our hearts while equipping and calling us to good works. (Paragraph 15)

✧ What is the opposite of faith? For some, it is a different faith: instead of believing in God, they believe in money, or pleasure, or power. For others, it is despair: they have given up on life. And for others, it is control: as long as they are in control, they don't need faith. Which of these forms of unbelief is a greater danger for you?

✧ Finally, take hold of Jesus. Call him in prayer to be present with you now. Allow his arms to hold you and his love to enfold you.
✦ How can you hold Jesus?
✦ How can Jesus touch you physically?
✦ Read Matthew 25:34–40. Now meditate on this thought: Faith is a reorientation of one's whole life.

God's Word

But now, apart from law, the righteousness of God has been disclosed, and is attested by the law and the prophets, the righteousness of God through faith in Jesus Christ for all who believe. For there is no distinction, since all have sinned and fall short of the glory of God; they are now justified by his grace as a gift, through the redemption that is in Christ Jesus, whom God put forward as a sacrifice of atonement by his blood, effective through faith. He did this to show his righteousness, because in his divine forbearance he had passed over the sins previously committed; it was to prove at the present time that he himself is righteous and that he justifies the one who has faith in Jesus.

Then what becomes of boasting? It is excluded. By what law? By that of works? No, but by the law of faith. For we hold that a person is justified by faith apart from works prescribed by the law. Or is God the God of Jews only? Is he not the God of Gentiles also? Yes, of Gentiles also, since God is one; and he will justify the circumcised on the ground of faith and the uncircumcised through that same faith. Do we then overthrow the law by this faith? By no means! On the contrary, we uphold the law. (Romans 3:21–31)

Closing prayer:

O Father and God of all comfort, through your word and Holy Spirit grant us a firm, glad, and grateful faith. By it may we easily overcome this and every other trial, and at length realize that what your dear Son Jesus Christ himself says is true, "But take courage; I have conquered the world" (John 16:33). Amen. (Brokering, p. 85)

✧ Meditation 5 ✧

Life in the Word

Theme: In a church overgrown with rules, customs, and ceremonies that were divorced from the Gospels and whose meaning had been dimmed over the centuries, Brother Martin found renewed life in the fountain of Christian truth, the Holy Bible.

Opening prayer: Dear God, give me a humble heart and open ears that in the words and stories of this ancient book, we today may hear you calling us to a new life.

About Martin

Emperor Charles V had condemned Martin as an outlaw. Pope Leo X had excommunicated the troublesome monk from the church. The Augustinians had released him from the community. He had suddenly become public enemy number one. Elector Frederick of Saxony correctly feared for Luther's safety and decided to spirit him away into a safe hiding place. So on Martin's return from the Diet of Worms, Frederick staged a kidnapping and Luther disappeared.

Many supporters feared that he was dead, and rumors flew about Germany. But Martin was not dead. He was safely stashed away in a fortress in the Thuringian forest known as the Wartburg. It was not far from his birthplace. Here Martin stayed for the next ten months, not particularly happy with his exile, this enforced sabbatical. But, ultimately, he used the time to begin what must rank among his most important accomplishments: the translation of the Bible into a lively, idiomatic German that would become a standard not only for biblical translation but also in the consolidation of a multitude of dialects into a common German tongue.

Father Martin's own pilgrimage from spiritual bondage to freedom had been enabled by the Holy Scriptures. The overwhelming complexity of canon law and scholastic theology only drove him deeper into confusion and despair. The out-and-out superstition that flourished among the masses of ordinary peasant-Catholics deeply distressed him, especially when the church's pastors seemed not to care, or worse, to manipulate superstition for profit.

But in his biblical studies, Martin found something else. He found the Gospel—clear, pure, direct, liberating. Instead of a labyrinth of rules and rationalism, he found the promise that God loved him and forgave him. He found a living Jesus reaching out to him from the cross. Luther could know this Jesus because as a highly educated priest, he could read Latin, Greek, and Hebrew. He had access to the great Bible chained to its stand in the monastery library.

In his great translation, Martin sought to make this sweet book available to everyone. He worked hard to make the translation meaningful for the peasants, the farmers, the merchants who walked the streets of Wittenberg. As Roland Bainton charmingly put it, "Judea was transplanted to Saxony, and the road from Jericho to Jerusalem ran through the Thuringian forest" (p. 257). Luther's Bible was not only a literary masterpiece but a spiritual Magna Carta.

Pause: How do you read the Bible? Do you use it as primarily a history of Israel and early Christianity or as a handbook for correct teachings? Or do you read it expecting and hoping to hear God addressing you with a living Word?

Martin's Words

This is a report of Luther's appearance before the emperor at Worms in 1521. The author is not known. It has been attributed to Luther and to a number of his associates, most plausibly to his close friend Justus Jonas, in collaboration with Martin; his lawyer at Worms, Jerome Schurf; and his friend Nicholas Amsdorf. Luther had been asked to recant his teachings. What follows is his answer with comments by the original author:

"Since then your serene majesty [Emperor Charles V] and your lordships seek a simple answer, I will give it in this manner, neither horned nor toothed: Unless I am convinced by the testimony of the Scriptures or by clear reason (for I do not trust either in the pope or in councils alone, since it is well known that they have often erred and contradicted themselves), I am bound by the Scriptures I have quoted and my conscience is captive to the Word of God. I cannot and I will not retract anything, since it is neither safe nor right to go against conscience.

"I cannot do otherwise, here I stand, may God help me, Amen." . . .

Dr. Martin replied humbly and modestly: He did not allow nor would he ever allow it to be said that he avoided the judgment of the emperor, the princes, and nobility of the empire. For so far was he from scorning their judgment that he would permit his works to be examined minutely and severely, on the condition that it be done by the authority of holy Scripture and the divine Word. For the Word of God was so clear to him that he was unable to yield unless taught better by the Word of God. For St. Augustine writes that he had learned that only those books which are called canonical should be given the honor of belief in their absolute truth, and that he believed the rest of the learned fathers, no matter how holy and sanctified, only if they wrote the truth.

St. Paul had written on this same point to the Thessalonians: "Test everything; hold fast what is good" [1 Thess. 5:21]; and to the Galatians: "Even if an angel comes from heaven and preaches something different, let him be accursed" [Gal. 1:8], and do not believe him. He [Luther], therefore, besought them all the more not to violate his conscience, bound as it was by the chains of Scripture and the holy Word, by forcing him to deny that clear Word of God. And in order to prove agreeable to them personally and before his imperial majesty, he said that in other respects he would do everything most obediently. (Forell, pp. 112–119)

Reflection

In an age of biblical literalism, fundamentalism, and legalism, it would be easy to misunderstand Martin's teaching about the Bible. He was not substituting one static, legal authority—the Bible—for another—the legal authority of the church vested in the pope or in councils. Luther's concept of biblical authority was dynamic, not static or legal. The Scriptures' authority was the Gospel with its ability to lead us to a living Word of truth, to Jesus, and to the cross. Lutheran theologian Werner Elert remarked, "For Luther the Word becomes authoritative because it judges, promises, and pardons. Acknowledgment of its authority is nothing else than letting oneself be judged and pardoned" (p. 196).

Luther did not read the Bible as a series of infallible statements lined up in a row, all equally valid. He read the Bible from the center out. The center is the Gospel revealed by Jesus' life, death, and Resurrection. The center is God's gracious will to save. Everything must be interpreted in the light of this center. Martin was aware that we could read the Bible in other ways. We could read it to support legalism and oppression. But this was to misread the Bible. He said, "If adversaries use scripture against Christ, then we put Christ against the scriptures" (Empie, Murphy, and Burgess, p. 129). The authority of the Bible is the Gospel, or as a popular Lutheran professor said often, "It is Jesus who makes a Bible of the Bible."

✧ Consider this little ditty taught to children in Christian education classes in days gone by:

Holy Bible, book divine,
Precious treasure, thou art mine.
Mine to tell me whence I came,
Mine to tell me who I am.

Ask yourself: What role does Holy Scripture play in my daily life?

✧ Luther saw the Bible not as information, but as address. Meditate on this: Am I willing to read the Bible as a book about me, calling me to repentance, offering me a new life?

✧ Katherine Koob was held hostage in the U. S. embassy in Tehran, tied to a chair and blindfolded. She kept herself sane by remembering passages from Holy Scripture that she had been required to memorize as a little girl in Sunday school. Close your eyes and imagine yourself in a similar circumstance. What verse or section of Scripture would you hold on to? Recite this verse or remember this story—turn it over in your mind—let it seep down deep.

✧ Brother Martin compared the Bible to the manger in the stable at Bethlehem. He said that we do not worship the straw or the wood, but we reverence it for what it holds because it contains Christ. Keep this truth in mind and quietly pray the old collect for Holy Scripture:

Blessed Lord, you speak to us through the Holy Scriptures. Grant that we may hear, read, respect, learn, and make them our own in such a way that the enduring benefit and comfort of the Word will help us grasp and hold the blessed hope of everlasting life, given us through our Savior Jesus Christ. (*Lutheran Book of Worship*, p. 47)

God's Word

Your word is a lamp to my feet
and a light to my path.

I have sworn an oath and confirmed it,
 to observe your righteous ordinances.
I am severely afflicted;
 give me life, O LORD, according to your word.
Accept my offerings of praise, O LORD,
 and teach me your ordinances.
I hold my life in my hand continually,
 but I do not forget your law.
The wicked have laid a snare for me,
 but I do not stray from your precepts.
Your decrees are my heritage forever;
 they are the joy of my heart.
I incline my heart to perform your statutes
 forever, to the end.

(Psalm 119:105–112)

Closing prayer:

Dear heavenly Father, say something. I will gladly remain silent and be a child and learner. If I should rule the church with my own knowledge, wisdom, and understanding, I would have been sunk long ago. Therefore, dear God, you guide and direct it. I will gladly forsake my point of view and understanding and let you rule alone through your Word. Amen. (Brokering, p. 89)

✧   Meditation 6   ✧

The Law and the Gospel

Theme: The law does not allow anyone to stand before God's wrath. The Gospel does not allow anyone to perish before God's grace.

Opening prayer: O Holy Spirit, give me the gift of discernment. Slavery is so easy, freedom is so hard! I keep thinking that the one is the other. Help me to know the difference.

About Martin

One of the most embarrassing moments in Martin Luther's life illustrates one of his fundamental beliefs: The law always boxes people in. It can never create the opening people need in order to really live.

One of Martin's most important supporters was Landgrave Philip of Hesse. But Philip was having a terrible problem. He had an unhappy marriage that had been forced upon him when he was only nineteen years old. For a while, Philip was content to have mistresses on the side, a common practice of the day. But after he was converted by Luther's new preaching, this option seemed no longer possible. He stopped receiving Holy Communion lest he damage his soul.

What options did Philip have? One possibility was a papal annulment, but Philip was now a Lutheran, and Father

Martin was opposed to the concept of annulments. Luther saw annulment as one of those legal loopholes, available if someone was rich and powerful enough, but a mockery of God's holy law. Luther was also dead set against divorce, especially because of Jesus' words on the subject in Saint Matthew's Gospel.

Pondering Scripture, Martin noticed that whereas annulment was unbiblical and divorce was antibiblical, polygamy was perfectly biblical. The patriarchs were all polygamists! So Luther advised Philip of Hesse to take a second wife, but to do it secretly because it would create a scandal if it got out. Of course, knowledge of Luther's advice did get out and created a terrible scandal. Luther had tried to solve Philip's problem by squeezing a legal solution out of the Bible, and failed both Philip and the church.

The law could show Philip that he was not doing right, but it could not make things right. Strict marriage laws could not deal with the real pain and suffering of his individual circumstances, but permissiveness threatened the sanctity of a fundamental institution.

Pause: What happens when you are a square peg and all the holes are round?

Martin's Words

But we know that when by faith we apprehend Christ himself in our conscience, we enter into a certain new law, which swalloweth up the old law that held us captive. As the grave in which Christ lay dead, after that he was risen again was void and empty, and Christ vanished away; so when I believe in Christ, I rise again with him, and die to my grave, that is to say, the law which held me captive: so that now the law is void, and I am escaped out of my prison and grave, that is to say, the law. Wherefore the law hath no right to accuse me, or to hold me any longer, for I am risen again. . . .

. . . To live to the law is to die to God; and to die to the law, is to live to God. These two propositions are clean contrary to reason, and therefore no crafty sophister or law-worker can understand them. But learn thou the true understanding thereof. He that liveth to the law, that is, seeketh to be justified by the works of the law, is and remaineth a sinner: therefore he is dead and condemned. For the law cannot justify and save him, but accuseth, terrifieth, and killeth him. . . . Now, to live unto God, is to be justified by grace or by faith for Christ's sake, without the law and works.

This is then the proper and true definition of a Christian: that he is the child of grace and remission of sins, which is under no law. (Dillenberger, pp. 119–120)

Reflection

Martin believed that what made a real theologian was not erudition or degrees hanging on the wall but the ability to properly distinguish law and Gospel. A good theologian, one wit put it, is a Doberman pinscher for the Gospel, sniffing out the subtle ways Gospel is turned into yet more law.

Grace, for Luther, is not a legal maneuver that wipes the slate clean of sins and then returns us to the domain of the law. Grace is a new way of life. In a letter to his close friend Philipp Melanchthon, Martin said, "Sin boldly, but believe and rejoice in Christ even more boldly" (Gritsch and Jenson, p. 139). Father Martin is urging us to take hold of life with both hands, even while knowing that we will make a mess of it a lot of the time. Amidst the imponderables and impossibles that much of our life consists of, Luther urges us to walk in the way of Christ: the way of compassion, love, and understanding. He wants us to rely on God's gracious presence in Christ to keep picking us up as we keep falling down. We can dare to keep falling down because grace will never tire of picking us up.

Meditate on the following meditations and after each one say silently, prayerfully, "The letter kills, but the Spirit gives life."

✧ The Law reveals the incompatibility of our ability and our obligation. So where do we go from here?

The letter kills, but the Spirit gives life.

✧ A reflection on healing:

I was working in a mental hospital caring for a young man who was gay. He was in the hospital not because he was gay but because he was suicidal because he was gay. After one suicide attempt, he sat with me in his room and sobbed out a single word, "Why?" I asked his psychiatrist what it would take to cure him of his suicidal depression. The doctor said, "He must learn to accept and love the person he is."

The letter kills, but the Spirit gives life.

✧ In Georges Bernanos's novel *The Diary of a Country Priest*, a young priest dies an early death after a ministry fraught with failure and rejection. He lies in the apartment of a friend who is a lapsed Christian. The friend is unable to find a priest to give the dying priest the final consolations of the church. The dying man says: "Does it matter? Grace is everywhere" (p. 255).

The letter kills, but the Spirit gives life.

✧ The Gestapo came to arrest Pastor Andre Trochme for smuggling Jews out of Vichy, France. Pastor Trochme invited the officers to sit down to supper with him and his family. He refused to treat them as Gestapo officers, but insisted on treating them as human beings, brothers in Christ.

The letter kills, but the Spirit gives life.

✧ A reading from *Crime and Punishment*, by Fyodor Dostoevsky:

Raskolnikov turned and looked at her with emotion. Yes, he had known it! She was trembling in a real physical fever. He had expected it. She was getting near the story of the greatest miracle and a feeling of immense triumph came over her. Her voice rang out like a bell; triumph and joy gave it power. The lines danced before her eyes, but she knew what she was reading by heart. At the last verse "Could not this Man which opened the eyes of the blind . . ." dropping her voice she passionately reproduced the doubt, the reproach and censure of the blind disbelieving Jews, who in another moment would fall at His feet as though struck by thunder, sobbing and believing. . . . "And *he, he*—too, is blinded and unbelieving, he, too, will hear, he, too, will believe, yes, yes! At once, now," was what she was dreaming, and she was quivering with happy anticipation.

"Jesus therefore again groaning in Himself cometh to the grave. It was a cave and a stone lay upon it.

Jesus said, Take ye away the stone. Martha, the sister of him that was dead, saith unto Him, Lord, by this time he stinketh: for he hath been dead four days."

She laid emphasis on the word *four.*

"Jesus saith unto her, Said I not unto thee that if thou wouldest believe, thou shouldest see the glory of God?

Then they took away the stone from the place where the dead was laid. And Jesus lifted up His eyes and said, Father, I thank Thee that Thou hast heard Me.

And I know that Thou hearest Me always; but because of the people which stand by I said it, that they may believe that Thou has sent Me.

And when He thus had spoken, He cried with a loud voice, Lazarus, come forth.

And he that was dead came forth."

(She read loudly, cold and trembling with ecstasy, as though she were seeing it before her eyes.)

"Bound hand and foot with graveclothes; and his face was bound about with a napkin. Jesus saith into them, Loose him and let him go.

Then many of the Jews which came to Mary and had seen the things which Jesus did believed on Him."

She could read no more, closed the book and got up from her chair quickly.

"That is all about the raising of Lazarus," she whispered severely and abruptly, and turning away she stood motionless, not daring to raise her eyes to him. She still trembled feverishly. The candle-end was flickering out in the battered candlestick, dimly lighting up in the poverty-stricken room the murderer and the harlot who had so strangely been reading together the eternal book. (Pp. 284–285)

The letter kills, but the Spirit gives life.

God's Word

As Jesus was walking along, he saw a man called Matthew sitting at the tax booth; and he said to him, "Follow me." And he got up and followed him.

And as he sat at dinner in the house, many tax collectors and sinners came and were sitting with him and his disciples. When the Pharisees saw this, they said to his disciples, "Why does your teacher eat with tax collectors and sinners?" But when he heard this, he said, "Those who are well have no need of a physician, but those who are sick. Go and learn what this means, 'I desire mercy, not sacrifice.' For I have come to call not the righteous but sinners." (Matthew 9:9–13)

Closing prayer:

Lord, it is for your honor and to your service that I now ask. Oh be praised and glorified. I plead, fully aware that you have glory, and that I am a poor, undeserving sinner. I cannot be without your help. You are willing and able to grant it to all who ask for it. Oh see my need and misery, and help me for your honor's sake. Amen. (Brokering, p. 11)

Paradox

Theme: Martin Luther tries to pull us beneath the surface of life and into the depths where our neat explanations and theories break apart in the face of the complex reality of the human soul.

Opening prayer: Dear God, the human heart is unknowable; my own heart is unknowable. I cannot even begin to see all that is there. But you, O God, have searched me and known me. You are the place where I can come home to myself.

About Martin

One of the most charming stories about Martin takes place on a stormy night. Two young Swiss students, traveling to Wittenberg to study under the great Dr. Luther, sought refuge at the Black Bear Inn in Jena. There, before the fire, they encountered a knight at his supper. But he was a strange knight, for he was reading the Hebrew Bible as he ate his dinner. The young men wondered if this was not the famous knight-humanist, Ulrich von Hutten. The innkeeper whispered to the students that he thought that the knight might be Dr. Luther himself.

The knight invited the students to eat with him, and they talked into the night, discussing unknightly topics such as Christ, grace, and the reform of the church. He told them that he was rather sure that Martin Luther was not currently in Wittenberg, but that they should try to study under Luther's close friend Professor Philipp Melanchthon.

The next morning, as the knight was preparing to mount his horse and travel on, the young Swiss students summoned up their courage and asked him, "Is it true that you are the great knight, Ulrich von Hutten?" The innkeeper, who was standing by, interrupted, "I tell you he is not von Hutten! This is Doctor Luther." The knight laughed at them all: "One says I'm von Hutten. One says I'm Luther. Who knows, maybe I'm the devil!" And he rode off.

This intriguing story is actually symbolic both of the complexity of Martin and of our complex reactions to him. He was one of the greatest geniuses of Western civilization: a man who changed the course of history. But he could also be small, petty, vindictive. He was a person of astonishing erudition and culture. And he could be revoltingly coarse and hateful. He was gregarious, generous, humorous, and prodigiously talented. And he was mean-spirited, anti-Semitic, and neurotic.

The Martin Luther who declared, "Here I stand," in rebellion against the emperor and the pope is the same Luther who declared during the Peasants' Revolt: "Let everyone who can, smite, slay, and stab, secretly or openly, remembering that nothing can be more poisonous, hurtful, or devilish than a rebel. It is just as when one must kill a mad dog; if you don't strike him, he will strike you, and the whole land with you" (Bainton, p. 217).

The dark side of Father Martin's character may surprise and disturb us, but it is also the real source of Luther's true greatness and of his most important insights. Martin was devastatingly aware of his dark self. This awareness drove him to the core of the human soul and to the knowledge that his salvation could come only from God, by grace alone.

Pause: Ever since Socrates, virtually all the great philosophers, mystics, and sages of the world have agreed that the most important, but also the most elusive, knowledge is knowledge of our true self. Why is this so?

Martin's Words

When I was a monk I thought by and by that I was utterly cast away, if at any time I felt the concupiscence of the flesh: that is to say, if I felt any evil motion, fleshly lust, wrath, hatred, or envy against any brother. I assayed many ways, I went to confession daily, &c., but it profited me not; for the concupiscence of my flesh did always return, so that I could not rest, but was continually vexed with these thoughts: This or that sin thou hast committed; thou art infected with envy, with impatiency, and such other sins; therefore thou art entered into this holy order in vain, and all thy good works are unprofitable. If then I had rightly understood these sentences of Paul: 'The flesh lusteth contrary to the spirit, and the spirit contrary to the flesh,' &c. and 'these two are one against another, so that ye cannot do the things that ye would do,' I should not have so miserably tormented myself, but should have thought and said to myself, as now commonly I do: Martin, thou shalt not utterly be without sin, for thou hast yet flesh; thou shalt therefore feel the battle thereof, according to that saying of Paul: 'The flesh resisteth the spirit.' Despair not therefore, but resist it strongly, and fulfill not the lust thereof. Thus doing thou art not under the law.

I remember that Staupitius was wont to say: 'I have vowed unto God above a thousand times, that I would become a better man; but I never performed that which I vowed. Hereafter I will make no such vow: for I have now learned by experience, that I am not able to perform it. Unless therefore God be favourable and merciful unto me for Christ's sake, and grant unto me a blessed and a happy hour when I shall depart out of this miserable life, I shall not be able with all my vows and all my good deeds, to stand before him.' This was not only a true, but also a godly and a holy desperation: and this must they all confess both with mouth and heart, which will be saved. (Dillenberger, pp. 148–149)

Reflection

Martin's understanding of the Christian faith is based on two fundamental paradoxes. The greatest paradox we will examine in our final meditation: The God who saves us by dying, raises us up by making himself low. But this great paradox of salvation is founded upon an equally strange truth about the human heart. Even Christians, Luther insisted, are always "sinful and holy at the same time, an enemy and a son of God" (Elert, p. 59).

Martin was trying to make a space for honesty about souls in between the legalism of the late medieval church and the moralism of the rising Calvinist Protestantism. He recognized, especially based on a deep and unvarnished inspection of his own life, that we cannot divide people into neat categories: white hats and black hats, good and evil.

We are holy by God's grace, which looks past our sinfulness to a new possibility. We are children of God because God does not allow the enemy of God to have the last word. Our Creator sees back to our creation in God's own image and renews that image, hidden though it may be beneath aeons of rebellion. Like Lazarus rising from the tomb by the word and love of Jesus, by Jesus our true self stirs and rises from the land of death.

✧ When we go to church, we often hear so much about who we ought to be that it discourages us from facing who we are. A good spiritual director will require you to set aside the question Who should I be? until you have clearly asked the question Who am I? In conversation with Jesus, hear him pose that question to you. Answer it the best way you can right now. Ask the question in conversation with Jesus regularly. Particularly explore all the wonderfully mysterious paradoxes of your life.

✧ One way to get in touch with the real self is through a journal. Robert Frost said, "For me the initial delight [in writing] is in the surprise of remembering something I didn't know I knew." Many have discovered that as they write, surprising truths turn up on the page because we are always writing over the edge of our consciousness. Just start writing about what happened in your life today and how the day felt. Consider making this a regular part of your prayer life. Open yourself to the paradoxes.

✧ Ask, Who is my secret self? Consider the self you would not want friends and family to know about. What effect does he or she have on your faith life? Can you learn to be this person before God?

✧ Critics have long recognized that sentimental art makes us out to be better than we really are, nihilistic art makes us out to be worse than we really are, and good art sees the human reality in its ambiguous wholeness. Martin Luther applied these standards to the church. How does the church of your experience measure up? Sentimental? Judgmental? Or is it one of those rare places where you and others can be whole?

✧ Read some poetry. Contemplate a great painting. Listen to a piece of really good music. There are truth tellers, both in the church and in the general culture. Why do we avoid them? Dare we listen to poems of paradox like this one by Emily Dickinson?

> Success is counted sweetest
> By those who ne'er succeed.
> To comprehend a nectar
> Requires sorest need.
>
> Not one of all the purple Host
> Who took the Flag today
> Can tell the definition
> So clear of Victory
>
> As he defeated—dying—
> On whose forbidden ear
> The distant strains of triumph
> Burst agonized and clear!

(Johnson, p. 7)

God's Word

Then Jesus, again greatly disturbed, came to the tomb. It was a cave, and a stone was lying against it. Jesus said, "Take away the stone." Martha, the sister of the dead man, said to him, "Lord, already there is a stench because he has been dead four days." Jesus said to her, "Did I not tell you that if you believed, you would see the glory of God?" So they took away the stone. And Jesus looked upward and said, "Father, I thank you for having heard me. I knew that you always hear me, but I have said this for the sake of the crowd standing here, so that they may believe that you sent me." When he had said this, he cried with a loud voice, "Lazarus, come out!" The dead man came out, his hands and feet bound with strips of cloth, and his face wrapped in a cloth. Jesus said to them, "Unbind him, and let him go." (John 11:38–44)

Closing prayer:

O Father, relieve our consciences, now and in the hour of death, from the terror of our guilt and the fear of your judgment. Let your peace come into our hearts that we may await your judgment with joy. Be not severe in your judgment of us, or no one will be found righteous. Teach us, dear Father, not to trust or find comfort in our own merits or good works. But teach us to venture and resign ourselves faithfully and firmly to your infinite mercy. In the same manner let us not lose courage because of our sinful and guilty lives. Let us regard your mercy as higher and broader and stronger than all our being. Amen. (Brokering, p. 35)

The Sacraments

Theme: This life is a long, hard journey to the Kingdom of God. The church is a pilgrim on the journey. The sacraments are our provisions for the journey. They are means of grace by which God sustains us.

Opening prayer: We thank you, Jesus, that as we travel through this wilderness, you are really present with us and for us in the holy sacraments.

About Martin

In 1529, Philip of Hesse invited Martin and the other leaders of the Reformation, especially the Swiss reformers Ulrich Zwingli and John Oecloampadius, to a conference at his castle in Marburg. Philip was interested in forging a military alliance among the various strands of the Reformation. Luther suspected military alliances, and he was concerned that true Gospel teaching not be sacrificed for political expediency. The issues dividing the house were the place of the sacraments in the life of the church, and especially belief in the real presence of Jesus Christ, as true God and true Man, in the sacrament of Holy Communion.

Luther began dramatically. He took a piece of chalk and wrote the Latin words *Hoc est corpus meum,* "This is my body," on the conference table around which they were all sitting, and then he drew a circle around the words. The challenge was clear. Until the various strands of the Reformation could agree on the meaning of these words, they could not be one church.

It turned out that they could not agree. For Zwingli, the sacrament was a memorial of an absent Christ. "This is my body" meant "This signifies my body." Oecloampadius was willing to grant a spiritual presence of Christ, but not a physical one since the spiritual and the fleshly were, to his mind, antithetical.

Luther insisted that this was not so. The whole point of the sacraments is their materiality. The sacraments are incarnation events: God comes to us in terms of our corporeal reality. It is the only reality we know. Jesus is really present in the bread and the wine of Holy Communion and in the water of Baptism just as he was really present in the flesh, blood, and bone of the carpenter from Nazareth.

Pause: The people are leaving their pews and streaming toward the altar. Hearing is not enough. They are hungry and thirsty for the Word of God. Is this true for you?

Martin's Words

But you should let others recount the various benefits of hearing mass. Give it your attention that you may say and believe, with the prophet, that here is a table which has been made ready for you by God in the face of all who cause you anxiety, and at which your faith may feed and grow strong [Ps. 23:5]. Your faith feeds only on the word of the divine promise, for "man doth not live by bread alone, but by every word that proceedeth out of the mouth of God" [Matt. 4:4; Deut. 8:3]. Hence, at mass, you ought, first of all, to be a most minute observer of the words of the promise, as forming the richest banquet, with every variety of food and holy nourishment. You must esteem it greater than all else, trust in it above all else, cleave to it most firmly in spite of every sin, and unto death. If you do so, you will obtain not only those tiny drops and crumbs of fruits of the mass, which some have fabricated superstitiously, but the principal fountain of life itself. By this I mean faith in the very word, the source of all good; as it says in John 4 [John 7:38], "He that believeth in me, out of his belly shall flow living waters"; and again: "Whosoever drinketh of the water that I shall give him, there shall be in him a well of living water springing up into eternal life" [John 4:14].

Now there are two defects from which we commonly suffer, and which prevent our understanding the fruits of the mass. The first is that we are sinners; and our profound unworthiness makes us unfit for such great things. Secondly, even if we were worthy, these things are so highly exalted that our timorous nature would not dare either to seek or to hope for them. Forgiveness of sins and eternal life!—who would not be overawed by them, rather than dare to hope for them, if the great benefits issuing from them were given their due importance. By them, we may have God as our Father, and ourselves become sons and heirs of all God's riches. To outweigh this twofold defect of our nature, we must lay hold of the word of Christ, and look to Him more steadily than to our sense of weakness. For great are the works of the Lord; they are all full of His purposes, and He is able to give beyond what we ask or think. If they did not exceed our worth, our capacity, and indeed every talent of ours, they would not be divine. Christ also encourages us in the same way when He says: "Fear not, little flock, for it is the Father's good pleasure to give you the Kingdom" [Luke 12:32]. This incomprehensible wealth of God, showered upon us through Christ, causes us to love Him, in return, most ardently and above all else. We are drawn to Him with the fullest confidence, despising all things else, and being made ready to suffer all things for Him. Thus the sacrament is aptly called "a fount of love." (Dillenberger, pp. 280–281)

Reflection

Lutheran theologian Eric Gritsch beautifully captured Martin's understanding of the sacraments when he said that for Luther, "The Lord's Supper is the combat ration of the church struggling to do God's will in the world" (Gritsch and Jenson, p. 75). This is why Martin could not accept the Swiss reformers' view that it is faith that makes Christ present in the sacraments. For Martin, faith does not bring about Christ's presence, rather Christ's presence in the sacraments makes faith possible. "My faith does not make the baptism but rather receives the baptism, no matter whether the person being baptized believes or not; for baptism is not dependent upon my faith but upon God's Word." Also, "I am a learned man and a preacher and I go to the sacrament in the faith of others and in my own faith. Nevertheless, I don't stand on that, I stand on [His words]: 'Take; this is my body'" (Dillenberger, p. 232).

All this reminds us again that the usefulness of Martin Luther as a spiritual guide is founded upon his intense awareness of how hard a thing faith is, of what a continuous and painful struggle the Christian life is. His hope was never centered in his ability to believe rightly or to live rightly. His hope was always in the God alive for us in Jesus, the God who gives himself to us in the sacraments, the God who forgives and loves and in forgiving and loving transforms us.

✧ Spiritualism is the bane of religion. Dualism causes us to try to be body-less Christians. The sacraments call us back to our body and to the struggle to be Christians in our real life. Meditate on your body: your physical body, your social body, your work body, your play body. See this body in all its dimensions as the sacramental place where God calls you to life in Christ.

✧ Don't let the brokenness, the fallibility, of your body oppress you. Remember that your body is Christ's. He has put a claim on it. Brother Martin writes, "To appreciate and use

Baptism aright, we must draw strength and comfort from it when our sins or conscience oppress us, and we must retort, 'But I am baptized! And if I am baptized, I have the promise that I shall be saved and have eternal life, both in soul and body'" (Tappert, p. 442). Prayerfully repeat these words, "My body is Christ's." Let the words plant seeds of acceptance in your soul.

✦ Are you a Christian? Our ancestors seemed to know for sure who was and who was not a believer, but in our day, the waters have become muddy and our thoughts confused. We're not so sure about the Bible as our forebears were. We find ourselves questioning our pastors and bishops. If "being a Christian" requires certainty and clarity and obedience, how many of us qualify? Father Martin writes: "How am I to know for certain that I belong to the people of God?" His answer: "We . . . have the Keys, Baptism, the Eucharist, and the promises of the Gospel" (Pelikan, *Luther's Works,* vol. 6, p. 10). In other words, *our* faith is not in our faith, but in God's promises, God's pledge or *sacramentum,* given to us over and over again in water, oil, bread, wine, and hands on our bowed head. Recall the most poignant moments of experience with the sacraments that you have had.

✦ We're tired. We're still in the wilderness, still on the journey. The sacraments accompany us and help us remember where we're going. Martin writes: "Thus this life is not piety; it is the process of becoming pious. It is not health; it is the process of becoming healthy. It is not being; it is becoming. It is not rest; it is activity. As yet we are not; we are becoming. It is not yet done and has not yet taken place; it is in the process of becoming. It is not the end; it is the way" (Elert, p. 299). Ponder Luther's words here, and then talk with Jesus about your experience of the journey; does it match Luther's?

God's Word

Jesus said to them, "I am the bread of life. Whoever comes to me will never be hungry, and whoever believes in me will never be thirsty. But I said to you that you have seen me and yet do not believe. Everything that [Abba] gives me will come to me, and anyone who comes to me I will never drive away; for I have come down from heaven, not to do my own will, but the will of [the One] who sent me. And this is the will of [the One] who sent me, that I should lose nothing of all that [God] has given me, but raise it up on the last day." . . .

Then the Jews began to complain about him because he said, "I am the bread that came down from heaven." They were saying, "Is not this Jesus, the son of Joseph, whose father and mother we know? How can he now say, 'I have come down from heaven'?" Jesus answered them, "Do not complain among yourselves. No one can come to me unless drawn by the [One] who sent me; and I will raise that person up on the last day. It is written in the prophets, 'And they shall all be taught by God.' . . . Very truly, I tell you, whoever believes has eternal life. I am the bread of life. Your ancestors ate the manna in the wilderness, and they died. This is the bread that comes down from heaven, so that one may eat of it and not die. I am the living bread that came down from heaven. Whoever eats of this bread will live forever; and the bread that I will give for the life of the world is my flesh." (John 6:35–51)

Closing prayer:

O my God, I am a sinner, and yet I am not a sinner. Alone and apart from Christ, I am a sinner. But in my Lord Jesus Christ and with him, I am no sinner. I firmly believe that he has destroyed all my sins with his precious blood. The sign of this is that I am baptized, cleansed by God's word, and declared absolved and freed from all my sins. In the sacrament of the true body and blood of my Lord Jesus Christ I have received as a sure sign of grace the forgiveness of sins. This he has won and accomplished for me by the shedding of his precious blood. For this I thank him in eternity. Amen. (Brokering, p. 77)

The First Table of the Ten Commandments

Theme: "Nothing but love fulfills the commandments, and nothing but self-love breaks them" (Fischer, p. 130).

Opening prayer: Help us, O God, to understand the Commandments, not as mere rules and regulations, but rather as a description of life lived Godward.

About Martin

By 1525, Saxony was a Lutheran state. But there was as yet no Lutheran church, no structure, no bishops, no seminaries. Luther began to urge the new elector, John Frederick, to establish a visitation of the parishes of Saxony to see what was going on there. These parishes were now in the Lutheran sphere of influence, but did that mean they understood the Lutheran preaching? One priest who lived near the boundary between Lutheran and Catholic territories reportedly served a parish on one side of the border according to the Lutheran rite and another on the other side according to the Roman!

The wheels turned slowly. Finally, in June of 1527, the guidelines for the visitation were drawn up. More time passed. More problems were argued out before things got under way.

Luther joined one of the visiting teams, which included four persons: two would examine the physical plants and financial conditions in these parishes, and two would focus on spiritual and theological concerns. Luther's team conducted its visits from 22 October 1528 until 9 January 1529.

What the visitors found in the parishes appalled Father Martin, to put it mildly. He described conditions this way:

> Good God, what wretchedness I beheld! The common people, especially those who live in the country, have no knowledge whatever of Christian teaching, and unfortunately many pastors are quite incompetent and unfitted for teaching. Although the people are supposed to be Christian, are baptized, and receive the holy sacrament, they do not know the Lord's Prayer, the Creed, or the Ten Commandments, they live as if they were pigs and irrational beasts, and now that the Gospel has been restored they have mastered the fine art of abusing liberty.
>
> How will you bishops answer for it before Christ that you have so shamefully neglected the people and paid no attention at all to the duties of your office? May you escape punishment for this! You withhold the cup in the Lord's Supper and insist on the observance of human laws, yet you do not take the slightest interest in teaching the people the Lord's Prayer, the Creed, the Ten Commandments, or a single part of the Word of God. Woe to you forever!
>
> I therefore beg of you for God's sake, my beloved brethren who are pastors and preachers, that you take the duties of your office seriously, that you have pity on the people who are entrusted to your care, and that you help me to teach the catechism to the people, especially those who are young. (Tappert, p. 338)

As a result of Martin's dismay, he wrote two of the most enduring documents of the Reformation: the *Small Catechism* of 1529 (originally published as posters) and the *Large Catechism*, a revision of catechetical sermons Martin preached in 1528 and 1529. Lutheran children studied and even memorized the *Small Catechism*. Luther originally intended it to be a simple form for parents to teach their children. As with his translation of the Bible, so also with the catechism, Martin effectively returned religion to the home. The *Small Catechism* is one of the great Christian classics, a literary and spiritual gem.

Pause: Ponder these words of Luther:

Let all Christians exercise themselves in the Catechism daily, and constantly put it into practice, guarding themselves with the greatest care and diligence against the poisonous infection of such security or vanity. Let them continue to read and teach, to learn and meditate and ponder. Let them never stop until they have proved by experience that they have taught the devil to death and have become wiser than God himself and all his saints. (Tappert, p. 361)

Martin's Words

THE TEN COMMANDMENTS
*in the plain form in which the head of the family
shall teach them to his household*

The First
"You shall have no other gods."
What does this mean?
Answer: We should fear, love, and trust in God above all things.

The Second
"You shall not take the name of the Lord your God in vain."
What does this mean?
Answer: We should fear and love God, and so we should not use his name to curse, swear, practice magic, lie, or deceive, but in every time of need call upon him, pray to him, praise him, and give him thanks.

The Third
"Remember the Sabbath day, to keep it holy."
What does this mean?
Answer: We should fear and love God, and so we should not despise his Word and the preaching of the

same, but deem it holy and gladly hear and learn it. (Tappert, p. 342)

Reflection

Following the Catholic tradition, Martin divided the Ten Commandments into two tables. The first table, commandments 1, 2, and 3, defined our proper relationship with God; whereas the second table, commandments 4 to 10, outlined proper behavior toward our neighbor.

The two tables are, of course, closely related. The reason we need the second table at all is that we have lost the relationship with God described in the first table. In his discussion of the first commandment in the *Large Catechism,* Martin claims, "Where the heart is right with God and this commandment is kept, fulfillment of all the others will follow of its own accord" (Tappert, p. 371). He describes the greatest breech of the second commandment to be false preaching. He says that the greatest offense against the third commandment is not failing to go to Mass but when "we permit ourselves to be preached to and admonished but we listen without serious concern" (Tappert, p. 378).

In other words, the issue is not works but faith. Once we misplace or misdirect our faith, everything else goes wrong. And, Martin is sure, we misdirect our faith on purpose. The reason we fail to love God above all things is that "all things" include us! Martin says that we do not get rid of God. Our strategy is much more devious. We turn God into an idol that Martin calls an apple-God, so that we can set up ourselves as God. An idol is a surrogate for the self. Using the following, meditate on your relationship with God:

✧ Luther believed (incorrectly it turns out) that the German word for *God* and the word for *good* were etymologically cognate. God is the one reality that wills only good. "He wishes to turn us away from everything else, and draw us to himself, because he is the one, eternal good" (Tappert, p. 366). Consider then, Why do we resist God?

✧ If it is true that _God_ is not a <u>noun</u>, _God_ is a <u>verb</u>, and the v<u>erb is _love,_</u> then what are commandments 1, 2, and 3 calling us to?

✧ Martin says that the problem with the second commandment is not that we swear at God when we stub our toe on the bedpost, but that we "attempt to embellish [ourselves] with God's name" (Tappert, p. 372). The Aryan Christians of the Nazi period and the so-called survivalist Christians of today exemplify this; they try to embellish their shameful deeds by cloaking themselves in God's name. But what of us? We also bear the name of Christ. Consider your own betrayals. Who is your apple-God?

✧ Father Martin believed that the biggest Sabbath breakers are in church. He wants to change the subject, asking not, "Do I go to church?" but, "How do I go to church?" "Why do I go to church?" and "Am I hoping for a life-changing word of God, or am I fulfilling a duty and keeping God safely in a box?" Pose these questions to yourself.

✧ Martin is confident that if we carefully and honestly compare ourself with the vision of the first three commandments, we will find cause for alarm. His purpose, however, is not to distress us or to hammer us with guilt. The <u>law's m</u>ajor func<u>tion is to drive us to Ch</u>rist. As we contemplate our failings, Martin says to us, in effect, "Your failings are not the point. We break faith with God; yes, yes. But he remains faithful, even to the cross on which we will crucify him." How does the law compel you to Christ?

God's Word

Surely, this commandment that I am commanding you today is not too hard for you, nor is it too far away. It is not in heaven, that you should say, "Who will go up to heaven for us, and get it for us so that we may hear it and observe it?" Neither is it beyond the sea, that you should say,

"Who will cross to the other side of the sea for us, and get it for us so that we may hear it and observe it?" No, the word is very near to you; it is in your mouth and in your heart for you to observe.

See, I have set before you today life and prosperity, death and adversity. If you obey the commandments of the LORD your God that I am commanding you today, by loving the LORD your God, walking in his ways, and observing his commandments, decrees, and ordinances, then you shall live and become numerous, and the LORD your God will bless you in the land that you are entering to possess. But if your heart turns away and you do not hear, but are led astray to bow down to other gods and serve them, I declare to you today that you shall perish; you shall not live long in the land that you are crossing the Jordan to enter and possess. I call heaven and earth to witness against you today that I have set before you life and death, blessings and curses. Choose life so that you and your descendants may live, loving the LORD your God, obeying [God], and holding fast to [God]; for that means life to you and length of days, so that you may live in the land that the LORD swore to give to your ancestors, to Abraham, to Isaac, and to Jacob. (Deuteronomy 30:11–20)

Closing prayer:

O my God and Lord, help me by the grace to learn and understand thy commandments more fully every day and to live by them in sincere confidence. Preserve my heart so that I shall never again become forgetful and ungrateful, that I may never seek after other gods or other consolation on earth or in any creature, but cling truly and solely to thee, my only God. Amen, dear Lord God and Father. Amen. (Brokering, p. 51)

The Second Table of the Ten Commandments

Theme: "A Christian is a perfectly free lord of all, subject to none. A Christian is a perfectly dutiful servant of all, subject to all" (Dillenberger, p. 53).

Opening prayer: Help us to see, loving God, that the purpose of the law is not the law, not obedience, not righteousness. The purpose of the law is to turn us in love toward our neighbor.

About Martin

Early on in the Reformation, it became clear that Martin's teaching that we are justified by faith, not by law, could be misinterpreted to be an invitation to lawlessness. Luther believed that this was exactly what was happening in the events that led up to the terrible Peasants' Revolt of 1524 to 1525.

Martin wanted to reform the Catholic church, and this would also necessarily bring about social reforms in a world where the church was the dominant institution. But others believed that reform was inadequate. They desired a revolution. Andrew Carlstadt, an early friend and supporter of Luther's, was one of these. He wanted to radically change the church:

eliminate music, clergy, art, and drastically alter the understanding of the sacraments. Carlstadt also wanted to change the world by enforcing a plain and simple life for all.

An even more radical figure, the brilliant preacher and visionary Thomas Muentzer, sought to do away with the sacraments altogether. He attacked the authority of Holy Scripture. To replace the sacraments and Scripture, he proposed that the new authority must be the Spirit-filled visionary, for example, himself. Muentzer then called for a violent revolution to overthrow the godless church and state of his time. He declared that the godless have no right to live.

The German peasants had virtually no rights. They suffered from oppression, hunger, and fear. At various times and places, peasants had risen against their overlords and against church authorities. Leaders like Muentzer gave a voice and vision to their anger.

Peasants all over the German lands began destroying castles and cloisters: 70 monasteries in Thuringia, 270 castles and 52 cloisters in Franconia. The rebellion claimed the lives and property of nobles, rich merchants, and churches. Not united by any single leader, with little or no organization, the peasants vented their long-standing grievances against the heavy oppression of both state and church.

Catholic princes and prelates blamed Luther for all of this tumult and for the uprisings that resulted. However, the teachings of people like Thomas Muentzer were as far from Luther's as possible. Martin knew that the Commandments were needed because without them society would collapse. He declared that the law could not be abolished unless and until sin had been abolished. He hated revolutions, he said, because they always leave a lot of people dead, and society no better, and perhaps, worse off than before. In his tract *Against the Murderous and Thieving Hordes of Peasants*, he wrote:

> If the peasant is in open rebellion, then he is outside the law of God, for rebellion is not simply murder, but it is like a great fire which attacks and lays waste a whole land. Thus, rebellion brings with it a land full of murders and bloodshed, makes widows and orphans, and turns everything upside down like a great disaster. (Bainton, p. 216)

Unfortunately, in his anxiety and terror, Martin appealed to the government to "smite, slay, stab" all the rebels. The princes were only too willing to oblige. Luther's intemperate language helped loose a bloodbath. During the ensuing suppression, as many as one hundred thousand peasants were killed. In horror, Luther remarked that the devils, driven from the rampaging peasants, instead of returning to hell, entered the government forces. Martin saw with his own eyes what happens when law gives way: first revolution, then vengeance. And always rivers of blood.

Pause: Northern Ireland. Algeria. Bosnia. Rwanda. Palestine. People abandon the norms of civilization in the name of a cause: sometimes a just cause, sometimes not. Ponder the result of believing that your cause permits you to violate God's law.

Martin's Words

The Fourth
"Honor your father and your mother."
What does this mean?
Answer: We should fear and love God, and so we should not despise our parents and superiors, nor provoke them to anger, but honor, serve, obey, love, and esteem them.

The Fifth
"You shall not kill."
What does this mean?
Answer: We should fear and love God, and so we should not endanger our neighbor's life, nor cause him any harm, but help and befriend him in every necessity of life.

The Sixth
"You shall not commit adultery."
What does this mean?
Answer: We should fear and love God, and so we should lead a chaste and pure life in word and deed, each one loving and honoring his wife or her husband.

The Seventh

"You shall not steal."

What does this mean?

Answer: We should fear and love God, and so we should not rob our neighbor of his money or property, nor bring them into our possession by dishonest trade or by dealing in shoddy wares, but help him to improve and protect his income and property.

The Eighth

"You shall not bear false witness against your neighbor."

What does this mean?

Answer: We should fear and love God, and so we should not tell lies about our neighbor, nor betray, slander, or defame him, but should apologize for him, speak well of him, and interpret charitably all that he does.

The Ninth

"You shall not covet your neighbor's house."

What does this mean?

Answer: We should fear and love God, and so we should not seek by craftiness to gain possession of our neighbor's inheritance or home, nor to obtain them under pretext of legal right, but be of service and help to him so that he may keep what is his.

The Tenth

"You shall not covet your neighbor's wife, or his manservant, or his maidservant, or his ox, or his ass, or anything that is your neighbor's."

What does this mean?

Answer: We should fear and love God, and so we should not abduct, estrange, or entice away our neighbor's wife, servants, or cattle, but encourage them to remain and discharge their duty to him. (Tappert, pp. 343–344)

Reflection

Martin believed that the commandments of the second table were really only one commandment: "Christ never gave any other commandment than that of love" (Dillenberger, p. 18). Martin said that we are not put on earth to serve God; God needs no service. We were put on earth to serve our neighbor. So Martin's analysis of the Commandments is generally quite uniform. His explanation of the the fifth commandment serves as a good example:

1. The motive for obedience: "We should fear and love God, so that . . ."
2. The negative obedience: "We should not endanger our neighbor's life or cause him any harm."
3. The positive obedience: "but help and befriend him in every necessity of life."

When Martin encouraged his barber, Master Peter, to pray the catechism each day, he was inviting him to do a daily reality check: How am I doing in my Christian journey from self-centeredness to love-centeredness? In the meditations that follow, use the Commandments and Luther's simple explanations as guides.

✧ Martin claimed that the fourth commandment is the most important in the second table because the family is the basic building block of society. "Out of the authority of parents all other authority is derived and developed" (Tappert, p. 384). The law protects us from chaos. The family is the front line. Meditate on the health of your family.

✧ The fifth commandment prohibits killing. Luther, like Saint Augustine, believed that violence was sometimes necessary for self-defense, but he knew that violence never solved anything. Do we know that? Why do so many people believe that the answer to criminal violence is state violence? Why do so many people believe that peace can be achieved through war?

✧ Martin wrote that "flesh and blood remain flesh and blood, and the natural inclinations and stimulations have their way without let or hindrance" (Tappert, p. 393). Healthy marriages depend on our accepting human sexuality as a good gift of God: (1) good, (2) gift, (3) of God. How are you doing?

✧ You shall not steal. Martin asks us to look at poor people, then to ask yourself: Does our country obey the seventh commandment? Do I?

✧ Regarding the eighth commandment, Martin comments: "There is nothing about a man or in a man that can do greater good or greater harm, in spiritual or in temporal matters, than this smallest and weakest of his members, the tongue" (Tappert, p. 404). This day, how have you used your tongue to harm another person? To offer consolation, praise, or thanks?

✧ Luther says that the ninth and tenth commandments provide the motivation for breaking the Commandments. The motive for obedience is that we fear and love God. The motive for disobedience is a self-love propelling us deep into envy. If we do not control our desire, it will control us. Examine yourself concerning envy and desire. How are you doing?

God's Word

My little children, I am writing these things to you so that you may not sin. But if anyone does sin, we have an advocate with the Father, Jesus Christ the righteous; and he is the atoning sacrifice for our sins, and not for ours only but also for the sins of the whole world.

Now by this we may be sure that we know him, if we obey his commandments. Whoever says, "I have come to know him," but does not obey his commandments, is a liar, and in such a person the truth does not exist; but whoever obeys his word, truly in this person the love of God has reached perfection. By this we may be sure that we are in him: whoever says, "I abide in him," ought to walk just as he walked. (1 John 2:1–6)

Closing prayer:

Lord God, I have indeed transgressed your commandments. I have been impatient in reverses and trials. I am unsympathetic and unmerciful. I do not help my neighbor. I am unable to resist sin. I do not tire of doing wrong. Dear Lord, pour out your grace to me and give me your Holy Spirit so that I may be obedient and keep each of your commandments. Help me to be at odds with the world and to give my heart and soul to you. Amen. (Brokering, p. 83)

✦ Meditation 11 ✦

The Lord's Prayer

Theme: We do not pray in order to change God's mind; we pray so that God can change our mind, our heart, our life.

Opening prayer: Take me to the place of prayer, dear God, where the world is bathed in the pure light of your presence.

About Martin

What was the young student Martin Luther thinking about on that hot summer day in 1505 as he made his way back to the University of Erfurt after a visit to his parents in Mansfeld? He had earned his baccalaureate degree and his master's degree and had just begun the study of the law. He had probably begun to memorize the titles of the laws from his copy of the *Corpus Iuris.*

Martin did not particularly want to be a lawyer; in fact, he held a lifelong prejudice against lawyers. He had often heard stories of lawyers repenting their wasted lives on their death beds and exclaiming, "O, that I had become a monk!" But Martin's father, Hans, had his heart set on his brilliant son becoming a lawyer to the benefit of the whole family. A marriage to a rich wife would inevitably follow. In the early sixteenth century, a young man obeyed his father's wishes.

Martin had been a sensitive child. He had been raised in a pious and superstitious home. He knew that God was a dangerous, angry God who needed to be placated with good works and special religious observances. Even God's Son was often portrayed with a sword coming out of his mouth. The saints, especially the Blessed Virgin, were needed to help the poor sinner win God's favor.

The plague had recently visited Erfurt. Three prominent men, all lawyers, had perished among many others. Was young Martin, with his sensitive heart, thinking over all these troubling things on that warm Wednesday afternoon in July? Was he resenting his father's demands? Was he contemplating the fearfulness of God? Was he thinking of how death comes so quickly and snatches us away?

As he walked along, deep in thought, perhaps he did not notice the thunderheads rolling in, but suddenly darkness surrounded him and the wind roared through the trees. Then a bolt of lightning hurled Martin to the ground. He felt sure that he had been shown the fearsome wrath of God. He prayed. He turned to the patron saint of miners (his father was a copper miner), who also helped those in danger of sudden death, Saint Anne, the mother of the Blessed Virgin. He cried out: "Help, Saint Anne. I will become a monk!"

Pause: Can you think of a time when life shocked you, tore away all the usual supports, and you turned to prayer as your sole refuge? When suddenly there was only prayer?

Martin's Words

Master Peter, Luther's barber, asked Martin questions about prayer. Martin answered in writing:

Dear Master Peter: I will tell you as best I can what I do personally when I pray. May our dear Lord grant to you and to everybody to do it better than I! Amen.

First, when I feel that I have become cool and joyless in prayer because of other tasks or thoughts (for the flesh and the devil always impede and obstruct prayer), I take my little psalter, hurry to my room, or, if it be the day and hour for it, to the church where a congregation is assembled and, as time permits, I say quietly to myself and word-for-word the Ten Commandments, the Creed, and, if I have time, some words of Christ or of Paul, or some psalms, just as a child might do.

It is a good thing to let prayer be the first business of the morning and the last at night. Guard yourself carefully against those false, deluding ideas which tell you, "Wait a little while. I will pray in an hour; first I must attend to this or that." Such thoughts get you away from prayer into other affairs which so hold your attention and involve you that nothing comes of prayer for that day.

It may well be that you may have some tasks which are as good or better than prayer, especially in an emergency. There is a saying ascribed to St. Jerome that everything a believer does is prayer and a proverb, "Those who work faithfully pray twice." This can be said because believers fear and honor God in their work and remember the commandment not to wrong anyone, or to try to steal, defraud, or cheat. Such thoughts and such faith undoubtedly transform their work into prayer and a sacrifice of praise. . . .

Yet we must be careful not to break the habit of true prayer and imagine other works to be necessary which, after all, are nothing of the kind. Thus at the end we become lax and lazy, cool and listless toward prayer. The devil who besets us is not lazy or careless, and our flesh is too ready and eager to sin and is disinclined to the spirit of prayer.

When your heart has been warmed by such recitation to yourself [of the Ten Commandments, the words of Christ, etc.] and is intent upon the matter, kneel or stand with your hands folded and your eyes toward heaven and speak or think as briefly as you can: . . .

O heavenly Father, dear God, I am a poor unworthy sinner. I do not deserve to raise my eyes or hands toward you or to pray. But because you have commanded us all to pray and have promised to hear us and through your dear Son Jesus Christ have taught us both how and what to pray, I come to you in obedience to your word, trusting in your gracious promise. I pray in the name of my Lord Jesus Christ together with all your saints and Christians on earth as he has taught us:

Our Father in heaven.

Hallowed be your name.

Your kingdom come.

Your will be done on earth as in heaven.

Give us today our daily bread.

And forgive us our sins, as we forgive those who sin against us.

Save us from the time of trial.

And deliver us from evil. Amen.

(Brokering, pp. 41–43)

Reflection

The great American rabbi Abraham Joshua Heschel once said that to pray is to dream in league with God, to envision God's holy visions. Father Martin would probably agree. In his discussion of the Lord's Prayer in the *Small Catechism,* he formulated his explanations according to a three-part formula as he had done with the Ten Commandments. The three parts are as follows:

1. A statement that God will do what we are asking for anyway, even without our prayer.
2. Therefore, the reason we pray (for God's name to be hallowed, or his kingdom to come, etc.) is so that we might participate in God's will, that God's will might become our will.
3. A brief discussion of how this can come about in our lives as Christians: for instance, God's name is hallowed when his word is taught clearly and we live by it.

So let us now try to pray the Lord's Prayer so that it also becomes our prayer. Using Jesus' words, let us try to dream the dream of God.

✦ *Our Father* in heaven. Close your eyes and climb into the lap of your father. Rest in his strong arms. Feel the safety of his love.

✦ *Hallowed* be your name. Orthodox Jews avoid uttering God's holy name lest they profane it. Is God's name too light on your lips? Martin suggests another way to hallow God's name: call upon God, cry out God's name, in every trouble, every joy, every day. "How sweet the name of Jesus sounds in a believer's ear."

✦ *Your* kingdom come. Ask yourself where and when the Kingdom of God has become visible on earth. Mother Teresa lifting up the dying in Calcutta? Albert Schweitzer working with lepers in the Congo? Martin Niemöller being held in a concentration camp because he stood up for Jews in Nazi Germany? What place is God providing in your community where you can reach out and make the Kingdom come?

✦ *Your* will be done on earth as it is in heaven. According to Saint John, God's will is that all humans be loved and become love. How can you be the agent of God's will? Close to you right now is someone who needs to be loved. Close to you right now is someone who wants to love you.

✦ *Give* us today our daily bread. Martin says that daily bread includes everything needed to satisfy bodily need, including good government and favorable weather. We enter this petition when we have thankful hearts for all our abundance and when we reach out to the poor and the hungry.

✦ *Forgive* us our sins as we forgive those who sin against us. This is the only conditional petition in the Lord's Prayer: forgive me as I forgive others. The Jesus revolution begins here. God creates a new community based not on wealth, education, goodness, perfection, or even fairness. The new world is founded on compassion. What acts of compassion are part of your Jesus revolution?

✧ *Save* us from the time of trial. Temptation is too light a word. This petition is about the ordeal, the great trial, the time of seduction and deception like Jesus' temptation in the wilderness. What trials do you need saving from?

✧ *Deliver* us from evil, literally, "from the evil One." Will love, peace, justice, forgiveness, and kindness prevail? Or will we fall again, for the big lie, for the rule of self, of greed, of power? Pray a litany, each sentence of which begins "Deliver us from . . ." and ends with an evil from which we need particular deliverance.

God's Word

First of all, then, I urge that supplications, prayers, inter-cessions, and thanksgivings be made for everyone, for kings and all who are in high positions, so that we may lead a quiet and peaceable life in all godliness and digni-ty. This is right and is acceptable in the sight of God our Savior, who desires everyone to be saved and to come to the knowledge of the truth. For
> there is one God;
>> there is also one mediator between God and
>> humankind,
> Christ Jesus, himself human,
>> who gave himself a ransom for all
—this was attested at the right time. For this I was ap-pointed a herald and an apostle (I am telling the truth, I am not lying), a teacher of the Gentiles in faith and truth.

I desire, then, that in every place the men should pray, lifting up holy hands without anger or argument. (1 Timothy 2:1–8)

Closing prayer: "Dear God, the woman of Canaan was a Gentile and was not among the chosen. As she did not let this hinder her from praying, I too will pray. I need help (and must have this and that). Where else could I look and find it but with you, through your Son, my Redeemer, Jesus Christ. Amen" (Brokering, p. 12).

✧ Meditation 12 ✧

Marriage and Family

Theme: God "honors and glorifies the married life, sanctioning and protecting it." It is a "glorious institution and an object of God's serious concern" (Tappert, p. 393). Martin Luther understood the need for intimate relationships and for family and how these are gifts from a loving God.

Opening prayer: Loving God, you give us all we need to sustain life, to make it flourish. Teach us to respond by thanking you, praising you, serving you, obeying you, for then this world will become, once again, a garden. In particular, help us do this by nurturing our families in their many different forms.

About Martin

Father Martin's preaching had broad results. His call to a new and free Christian life based on the Gospel's promises and in service of one's neighbors was being answered by large numbers of people. Many monks and nuns decided to leave their enclosures and take up new lives in the world of marriage, family, and daily work.

In the Nimbschen convent, near Grimma, about fifty miles south of Wittenberg, twelve of the nuns sent secret letters to their families, asking them for help in escaping from the convent. For such disobedience the nuns were caught and punished. Duke George even threatened to impose the death penalty on anyone abducting or luring nuns from their lawful places.

The Nimbschen nuns appealed for help to Martin in Wittenberg, and he arranged to have them rescued by a provisioner of the convent, one Leonard Koppe. Late at night on Holy Saturday in 1523, while most of the nuns slept before the start of the Great Vigil at midnight, Koppe made a delivery of herring. But when his wagon rumbled away from the convent, twelve nuns hid behind the empty herring barrels.

Suddenly, Martin found himself in the matchmaking business. Three of the sisters went home to their families. Martin found husbands or jobs as governesses for the others. One remained, Katherine von Bora. After the death of her mother, when Katherine was only nine years old, she had been sent to the convent. She was twenty-four when Luther rescued her. Two years later, the great Dr. Luther married her. Together they became a new model for Christian family life that would endure, especially in northern Europe, for centuries.

The local duke gave the couple the Augustinian cloister for their home. He also doubled Martin's salary. In the converted cloister, Katie and Martin had six children together and adopted four more. Katie's Aunt Magdalena, also an escapee from the convent, often lived with them. Twelve students from the university boarded with the Luthers. Each night at supper, Dr. Luther told stories as the students ate with one hand and took notes with the other. Sounds of music, laughter, and rampaging children filled the enormous house. One prince who was planning to visit the Luthers was warned that he would not be able to get any sleep in the boisterous Black Cloister of Wittenberg.

Luther could be strict but was considered somewhat liberal for his age. He disliked beating children, perhaps because of his own parents' severity. In his *Large Catechism,* he advised moderation: "This would be the right way to bring up children, so long as they can be trained with kind and pleasant methods, for those who have to be forced by means of rods and blows will come to no good end; at best they will remain good only as long as the rod is on their backs" (Tappert, p. 375).

The death of Martin's daughter Elizabeth before her first birthday nearly broke his heart. When his special favorite, Magdalena, died in his arms in her fourteenth year, Martin was inconsolable: "My dearest Magdalena has been reborn into Christ's eternal kingdom. . . . Yet though my wife and I ought only to rejoice and be thankful at such a happy journey and blessed end, we cannot. So strong is our love that we must sob and groan in heart under the power of killing grief" (Nohl, p. 115).

Pause: From the heart, pray for parents and children everywhere.

Martin's Words

On 22 August 1530, Luther wrote to his son Hans, then four years old:

> My dearest son:
>   I am glad to know that you learn well and pray hard. Keep on, my lad, and when I come home, I'll bring you a whole fair.
>   I know a lovely garden where many children in golden frocks gather rosy apples under the trees, as well as pears, cherries, and plums. They sing, skip, and are gay. And they have fine ponies with golden bridles and silver saddles. I asked the gardener who were these children, and he said, "They are the children who like to pray and learn and be good." And I said, "Good man, I too have a son, and his name is Hans Luther. Couldn't he come into the garden, too, and eat the rosy apples and the pears and ride a fine pony and play with these children?" And the man said, "If he likes to pray and learn and be good, he too may come into the garden and Lippus and Jost [the sons of Melanchthon and Jonas] as well; and when they all come together, they shall have golden whistles and drums and fine silver crossbows." But it was early, and the children had not yet had their breakfasts, so I couldn't wait for the dance. I said to the man, "I will go at once

and write all this to my dear son Hans that he may work hard, pray well, and be good, so that he too may come into this garden. But he has an Aunt Lena he'll have to bring too." "That will be all right," said he, "Go and write this to him."

So, my darling son, study and pray hard and tell Lippus and Jost to do this too, so that you may all come together into the garden. May the dear God take care of you. Give my best to Auntie Lena and give her a kiss for me.

Your loving father,
Martin Luther
(Bainton, pp. 236–237)

Reflection

During the era in which he lived, Martin sought to resist the spirit-body dualism that underlay so much of medieval religious practice. Instead, he affirmed our vocations in God's good creation, as fathers and mothers, as workers and craftspeople. In Luther's day, the term *vocation* had been pretty much restricted to priests and members of religious communities. Claiming that barbers, butchers, and farmers were called by God and that their work was as sacred as that of the clergy struck his contemporaries as radical.

In particular, the medieval notion that celibacy was a higher or holier way of life than marriage offended Martin. He believed that some people were called to be celibate, and their gift should be honored and nurtured, but not as a better or holier way of life. Marriage was, Luther insisted, "the most universal and the noblest estate." He called it "most richly blessed" (Tappert, p. 393). As such, marriage and family life in all its forms should be supported, affirmed, and nurtured as true paths to holiness.

✧ Do you ever fall victim to the notion that your bodiliness is less holy than your spirit? That your sexuality is less sacred than the life of the soul? How would God the Creator want us to view body and soul? Sexuality and intimacy?

✧ For married people: Think of some tangible thing you will do today so that your spouse will know that you are partners together in the flesh and blood of marriage. What can you do to express your thankfulness about your marriage?

✧ For single people: Meditate on how folks outside of "nuclear families" can remind everyone of all the other "families" we belong to: church families, neighborhood families, work families, a circle of friends, and so on. Offer God thanksgiving and praise for your families.

✧ For parent(s) and children: Think about glue. What is the glue that holds your family together? Do you need to apply more?

✧ Do something tangible to celebrate your marriage or your family life: make a special dinner and invite everyone just to come and celebrate.

God's Word

I consider that the sufferings of this present time are not worth comparing with the glory about to be revealed to us. For the creation waits with eager longing for the revealing of the children of God; for the creation was subjected to futility, not of its own will but by the will of the one who subjected it, in hope that the creation itself will be set free from its bondage to decay and will obtain the freedom of the glory of the children of God. We know that the whole creation has been groaning in labor pains until now; and not only the creation, but we ourselves, who have the first fruits of the Spirit, groan inwardly while we wait for adoption, the redemption of our bodies. (Romans 8:18–23)

Closing prayer:

Dear God, you have given to me my [spouse], children, house, and property. I receive these as you desire, and will care for them for your sake. Therefore I will do as much as possible that all may go well. If my plans do not all succeed, I will learn to be patient and let what cannot be changed take its course. If I do well I will give God the glory. I will say, O Lord, it is not my work or effort but your gift and providence. Take my place and be the head of the family. I will yield humbly and be obedient to you. Amen. (Brokering, pp. 94–95)

✧ Meditation 13 ✧

Redemption

Theme: When humanity turned away from God, life was transformed into death. We live in a world under the power of death. God in Christ enters death's realm and redeems us. Resurrection is the result.

Opening prayer: O gentle Jesus, humble of heart, you have bought us back with your own blood. In you we pass over from death to life, from sin to love, from Satan to God. Keep us safe in your redeeming love.

About Martin

The two young counts of Mansfeld were feuding again. For a third time in less than a year, Martin intervened to try to reconcile the brothers. Against Katherine's wishes, Luther set out for Eisleben on a bitterly cold winter day. He was accompanied by a servant, his secretary, and his three sons (Hans, nineteen; Martin, fourteen; and Paul, who would turn thirteen during the trip). The severe winter weather slowed their trip, so it took many days to reach Eisleben. During the three weeks of their stay, Luther mediated the quarrel, preached four times, and ordained two pastors. He felt ill the whole time. He often had chest pains and spells of dizziness.

On 17 February, after dinner, Martin retired early. He soon had the first of three heart attacks. His good friend Justus Jonas recorded the events of Martin's last journey. Doctors were, of course, summoned, and they applied warm compresses to his chest. Count Albert came with his wife and a "unicorn" horn. Scrapings from this, mixed in wine, were supposed to help. Martin slept off and on, but around two o'clock in the morning, he had a second attack. He told Justus, "I believe I'll stay in Eisleben, where I was born and baptized." Luther realized that he was dying, and several times during the night he repeated the same prayer: "Father, into your hands I commend my spirit. You have redeemed me, faithful God. Amen."

Luther had a third attack shortly after the second one and started to slip away. His old friend Justus leaned down close to the dying man and asked, "Reverend Father, are you willing to die in the name of Christ and the doctrine you have preached?" Martin's children and friends heard him softly but clearly respond, "Yes." Luther was dead at sixty-three years of age.

The counts of Mansfeld wanted to bury Father Martin there in the town of his birth, but they were overruled by the elector. Luther would be buried in the Castle Church, on whose doors he had nailed the Ninety-five Theses and changed the world. Thousands lined the roads from Eisleben to Wittenberg to honor the great Reformer. When the cortege neared Wittenberg, two of the duke's knights led sixty horsemen in front of the hearse. Martin's wife and children followed the casket, and behind them the faculty and students of Luther's university, the town council, and other dignitaries. The church and the square were jammed with people as Martin Luther was laid to rest not too far from the pulpit where he preached of a God whose love was stronger than death.

Pause: Repeatedly offer this prayer: Jesus, remember me when you come into your Kingdom.

Martin's Words

"And in Jesus Christ, his only son, our Lord: who was conceived by the Holy Spirit, born of the virgin Mary, suffered under Pontius Pilate, was crucified, dead, and buried: he descended into hell, the third day he rose from the dead, he ascended into heaven, and is seated on the right hand of God, the Father almighty, whence he shall come to judge the living and the dead."

What does this mean?

Answer: I believe that Jesus Christ, true God, begotten of the Father from eternity, and also true man, born of the virgin Mary, is my Lord, who has redeemed me, a lost and condemned creature, delivered me and freed me from all sins, from death, and from the power of the devil, not with silver and gold but with his holy and precious blood and with his innocent sufferings and death, in order that I may be his, live under him in his kingdom, and serve him in everlasting righteousness, innocence, and blessedness, even as he is risen from the dead and lives and reigns to all eternity. This is most certainly true. (Tappert, p. 345)

Reflection

Can we modern people, in our sophisticated, cynical, secular world, even begin to imagine the power words like *sin, death,* and *Satan* had for the people of Martin's day? And if we cannot, can we ever understand what the word *redemption* means? Fundamentalists may treat these as literal realities, whereas secularists may dismiss them as mere figures of speech.

Father Martin understood that sin, death, Satan, and redemption are spiritual realities. Behind greed, shallow self-centeredness, bigotry, injustice, and corruption of religion, he saw the spiritual principalities and powers of darkness. But, in the sacrificial love of God in Christ, he saw the spiritual power that defeats all our enemies.

In those last days before his death, Martin jotted down some notes on classical poetry and Christian life. The final words this extremely prolific writer would ever put down on paper were "We are beggars, it is true." We are beggars, it is true, but for us fights the valiant One, w<u>hom God elected</u>.

✧ Meditate on each stanza of Martin's most famous hymn, "A Mighty Fortress Is Our God." Sing one stanza, then take a few minutes of silent reflection, then go on to the next verse. Claim these strong words of promise for your own.

> A mighty fortress is our God,
> A sword and shield victorious;
> He breaks the cruel oppressor's rod
> And wins salvation glorious.
> The old satanic foe
> Has sworn to work us woe!
> With craft and dreadful might
> He arms himself to fight.
> On earth he has no equal.
>
> No strength of ours can match his might!
> We would be lost, rejected.
> But now a champion comes to fight,
> Whom God himself elected.
> You ask who this may be?
> The Lord of hosts is he!
> Christ Jesus, mighty Lord,
> God's only Son, adored.
> He holds the field victorious.
>
> Though hordes of devils fill the land
> All threat'ning to devour us,
> We tremble not, unmoved we stand;
> They cannot overpow'r us.
> Let this world's tyrant rage;
> In battle we'll engage!
> His might is doomed to fail;
> God's judgment must prevail!
> One little word subdues him.

God's Word forever shall abide,
No thanks to foes, who fear it;
For God himself fights by our side
With weapons of the Spirit.
Were they to take our house,
Goods, honor, child, or spouse,
Though life be wrenched away,
They cannot win the day.
The Kingdom's ours forever!

✧ Reread "Martin's Words" slowly, meditating on his statement of faith. Notice that Martin uses metaphors based on medieval images: castles and armies of knights. What metaphors would reflect your faith in the God who is at your side in life's dangerous conflicts? List these and meditate upon them.

✧ Ask yourself: How do I imagine death? What images does the word *death* evoke? Are they cold, dark images of "the end"? Or do I think of death as going to the Light? Luther thought of death as finally coming home to Jesus, to the arms of the one who understands, who loves, and who forgives.

God's Word

If God is for us, who is against us? . . . Who will bring any charge against God's elect? It is God who justifies. Who is to condemn? It is Christ Jesus, who died, yes, who was raised, who is at the right hand of God, who indeed intercedes for us. Who will separate us from the love of Christ? Will hardship, or distress, or persecution, or famine or nakedness, or peril, or sword? As it is written,
    "For your sake we are being killed all day long;
    we are accounted as sheep to be slaughtered."
No, in all these things we are more than conquerors through him who loved us. For I am convinced that neither death, nor life, nor angels, nor rulers, nor things present, nor things to come, nor powers, nor height, nor depth,

nor anything else in all creation, will be able to separate us from the love of God in Christ Jesus our Lord. (Romans 8:31–39)

Closing prayer: "Father, into your hands I commend my spirit. You have redeemed me, faithful God. Amen" (Brokering, p. 103).

✧　**Meditation 14**　✧

Sanctification
and the Church

Theme: Sanctification is what happens when, by the power of the Holy Spirit, people stop believing in the old world, and start living toward a new world, a world that grows up out of the cross of Jesus.

Opening prayer: Come, Holy Spirit. Make us into new people. Renew our hearts, change our minds, restore our hope, open our eyes, reignite our love. With your aid, and in Christ, we will be a new creation.

About Martin

Few men in Germany could match Luther's combination of erudition and eloquence, but there was at least one, and he was to become Luther's most formidable adversary. His name was John Eck, Dominican priest and professor of theology at the University of Ingolstadt. Before the publication of the Ninety-five Theses, he and Luther had been friends; afterward they were bitter enemies.

Eck had challenged Andrew Karlstadt to debate the new Wittenberg theology in a forum at the University of Leipzig, but he knew that Luther would come too. He debated

Karlstadt from 27 June into early July. Then, beginning on 4 July and going to 15 July, he debated Brother Martin. The topic of the debate with Martin was papal primacy, but both understood that the real issue was the nature of the one, holy, catholic, and apostolic church. Eck would later say that he and Luther could have resolved their differences on the other issues, but that the definition of the church was a difference of insuperable proportions.

Eck defended the medieval understanding of the church as an institution permanently configured by God and ruled and maintained by the pope as the vicar of Christ. Luther denied that the church was an institution at all, although it would always use institutions to carry out its mission. For Luther the church was a gathering of people by the Holy Spirit to hear and to teach the Gospel. The church is the assembly around word and sacrament. All the rest that we call church devolves from the eucharistic assembly.

Eck pounced on this assertion, accusing Martin of the heresy of John Hus, who had been burned at the stake a hundred years earlier. Luther responded:

> As for the article of Hus that "it is not necessary for salvation to believe the Roman Church superior to all others," I do not care whether this comes from Wyclif or from Hus. I know that innumerable Greeks have been saved though they never heard this article. It is not in the power of the Roman pontiff or of the Inquisition to construct new articles of faith. No believing Christian can be coerced beyond holy writ. (Bainton, p. 89)

Brother Martin was not denying that the church as an institution had a right to have a supreme head with broad powers. This was a human right that the church was using to organize effectively. However, the institutional church was not necessary for salvation, that is, by divine right. Eck rejected Martin's view because he correctly saw how this relativized the church's power and authority.

The debate at Leipzig in 1519 became one of the defining moments of the Reformation, not the least for Martin himself. He began to realize that he had started something that was much bigger than he had ever imagined. When Eck taunted

Luther, "Are you the only one that knows anything? Except for you is all the church in error?" Luther cringed (Bainton, p. 91). But he could not turn back.

His answer to Eck has been viewed as a signal of the coming of the modern age: "I want to believe freely and be a slave to the authority of no one, whether council, university, or pope. I will confidently confess what appears to me to be true, whether it has been asserted by a Catholic or a heretic, whether it has been approved or reproved by a council" (Bainton, p. 92).

Pause: Ponder authority. What is its source? What are its functions? What are its limits?

Martin's Words

When each person has forgotten himself and emptied himself of God's gifts, he should conduct himself as if his neighbor's weakness, sin, and foolishness were his very own. He should not boast or get puffed up. Nor should he despise or triumph over his neighbor as if he were his god or equal to God. Since God's prerogatives ought to be left to God alone, it becomes robbery when a man in haughty foolhardiness ignores this fact. It is in this way, then, that one takes the form of a servant, and that command of the Apostle in Gal. 5 [:13] is fulfilled: "Through love be servants of one another." Through the figure of the members of the body Paul teaches in Rom. 12 [:4–5] and I Cor. 12 [:12–27] how the strong, honorable, healthy members do not glory over those that are weak, less honorable, and sick as if they were their masters and gods; but on the contrary they serve them the more, forgetting their own honor, health, and power. For thus no member of the body serves itself; nor does it seek its own welfare but that of the other. And the weaker, the sicker, the less honorable a member is, the more the other members serve it "that there may be no discord in the body, but that the members may have the same care for one another," to use Paul's words [I Cor. 12:25]. From this it is now evident how one must conduct himself with his neighbor in each situation. (Dillenberger, pp. 91–92)

Reflection

Sanctification means "to make holy." A perennial issue in Christian thinking is how we become holy ones instead of sinners. Luther said, instead of asking how, ask where. The answer for Martin is that we cannot sanctify ourself, but the Holy Spirit sanctifies us in the place called church. The Holy Spirit "has led you into the holy, catholic church and placed you in the bosom of the church. But in that church he preserves [you] and through it he preaches and brings you [to Christ] through the Word" (Dillenberger, pp. 211–212). In the *Large Catechism,* Luther writes that the church "is the mother that begets and bears every Christian through the Word of God" (Tappert, p. 416).

Luther then reminds his people that the Greek word for *church* is "assembly." Don't, he said, translate *communio* as "communion," translate it "community." The church is not another organization, but a community of love and faith. It is not the Kingdom of God, but it is a people living toward the Kingdom of God in faith and hope.

✧ In our society, we admire people who are "self-made." Could this be why the church is so hard for modern people to understand? The church believes in Spirit-made people. It believes "self-made" is the problem. It asks us to forget self, to empty our self for neighbor. How are you doing?

✧ One of the reasons Martin had problems with the word *sanctification* is that it could lead people to believe that a church is a group of holy people instead of a gathering of sinners. We are holy only because we are forgiven: "Toward forgiveness is directed everything that is to be preached concerning the sacraments and, in short, the entire Gospel and all the duties of Christianity" (Tappert, p. 417). Do you think we would have more or less people coming to church if this were understood?

✧ Martin wrote: "Creation is past and redemption is accomplished, but the Holy Spirit carries on his work unceasingly until the last day. For this purpose he has appointed a community on earth, through which he speaks and does all his work" (Tappert, p. 419). In the sixteenth century, Martin feared that the church had nearly ceased being the Spirit's instrument. Is the modern church doing better? If so, where are we doing better? Where do we need to reform?

✧ People in Martin's day did good works in order to be saved, or to assist in salvation, or to work off time in purgatory. If all these reasons for doing good works are stripped away, what is left? Why do you do good things for other people?

✧ Read, slowly and carefully, this traditional prayer for the church. Ask God the Holy Spirit to show you how to make the prayer come true.

> Gracious Father, we pray for your holy catholic Church. Fill it with all truth and peace. Where it is corrupt, purify it; where it is in error, direct it; where in anything it is amiss, reform it; where it is right, strengthen it; where it is in need, provide for it; where it is divided, reunite it; for the sake of Jesus Christ, your Son our Savior. (*Lutheran Book of Worship*, p. 45)

God's Word

> I therefore, the prisoner in the Lord, beg you to lead a life worthy of the calling to which you have been called, with all humility and gentleness, with patience, bearing with one another in love, making every effort to maintain the unity of the Spirit in the bond of peace. There is one body and one Spirit, just as you were called to the one hope of your calling, one Lord, one faith, one baptism, one God and Father of all, who is above all and through all and in all. (Ephesians 4:1–6)

Closing prayer:

Almighty and everlasting Father of our Lord and Savior Jesus Christ, we see and feel how your church is doing in this world. We see its status and how it is annoyed in so many ways by the world and the devil. So we pray to you for the sake of your only begotten Son. First, comfort and strengthen our hearts by your Holy Spirit, so that we may not be overwhelmed by so many dangers. Also we pray that you will not only halt the purposes and plans of the enemies but will truly and marvelously help prove to the whole world that you care for the church. Rule, protect, and deliver it, ever living and reigning eternal God, God the Father, God the Son, and God the Holy Spirit. Amen. (Brokering, p. 78)

✧   **Meditation 15**   ✧

The Theology of the Cross

Theme: The death of Jesus on the cross is not merely the mechanism by which God saves us. The death of Jesus is the revelation of God. Who is God? God is the one who died on the cross.

Opening prayer: O God, in the holy cross, you become a God in total solidarity with suffering humanity. There, from the cross, you invite us to be human too.

About Martin

Martin wrote to his dear friend George Spalatin to say that he was unwilling to go to Worms to recant, but he was willing to go to die. The diet, or parliament, of the Holy Roman Empire was meeting in the spring of 1521 with the newly crowned emperor, the twenty-year-old Charles V.

Charles was unsure as to whether he should hear Luther. Both sides put pressure on him, and invitations were made and withdrawn. Finally, he decided to give Luther a hearing, but not to let him debate or even to explain himself. Luther was to be asked two questions:
1. Are these your books?
2. Will you recant what is in them?

Martin knew that his life was in serious danger as he rode to Worms, even though he traveled under the emperor's safe conduct. John Hus had been under a safe conduct when he went to the Council of Constance a century before, and he was arrested and burned at the stake anyway. The papal nuncio, Aleander, had openly demanded that Luther be taken into custody for a trial in Rome.

Luther was not the only nervous party at the diet. Everyone had something to lose if this issue were not handled just right. At issue was not just theology; Charles could not afford to alienate the Lutheran princes. Luther had popular support as well. Aleander reportedly said in great consternation, "Nine tenths of the Germans cried, 'Luther,' and the other one tenth, 'Death to the pope'" (Bainton, p. 130).

Nevertheless, on 18 April 1521, this common monk, son of a copper miner, found himself standing before the glittering court and austere dignity of the ruler of Germany, Austria, Spain, Burgundy, Luxembourg, the Netherlands, and parts of Italy. He had already been excommunicated by the pope. Now, he knew that he was in all probability going to fall under the terrible ban of the Holy Roman Emperor.

Perhaps he gathered courage by remembering the court of another king. Martin had been known to say that Jesus' courtiers were clothed with the cross. Martin was prepared to bear the cross for the sake of Christ. "My conscience is captive to the Word of God. I cannot and I will not recant anything, for to go against conscience is neither right nor safe. God help me. Amen" (Bainton, p. 144). Having defied the supreme authority in the church, he now defied the Holy Roman Emperor.

The emperor's response came weeks later in the Edict of Worms. Calling Martin a pagan, a beast, and a heretic, Charles declared Luther an outlaw. The law no longer protected him. He could be killed on sight. The emperor declared that his books should be eradicated from human memory.

Pause: It has been said that a person hasn't found something to live for until he or she has found what is worth dying for. Have you found the pearl of great price for your life?

Martin's Words

Through the regime of his humanity and his flesh, in which we live by faith, he makes us of the same form as himself and crucifies us by making us true men instead of unhappy and proud gods: men, that is, in their misery and their sin. Because in Adam we mounted up towards equality with God, he descended to be like us, to bring us back to knowledge of himself. That is the significance of the incarnation. That is the kingdom of faith in which the cross of Christ holds sway, which sets at naught the divinity for which we perversely strive and restores the despised weakness of the flesh which we have perversely abandoned. (Moltmann, pp. 212–213)

Reflection

The German theologian Jürgen Moltmann points out that the medieval mystics believed that we must take up the suffering of Christ and thus rise to God, a process known as divinization. We become like God through the cross.

Luther's theology, says Moltmann, "reverses this approach." Instead, God descends "to the level of our sinful nature and our death, not so that man is divinized, but so that he is de-divinized and given new humanity in the community of the crucified Christ" (p. 213). The Fall started when Adam and Eve desired to be like God, but Jesus comes to free us to be human beings again.

Martin showed scant interest in the old metaphysical "supreme being" of Aristotle and Thomas Aquinas. Martin's God is not all-powerful, but broken and dying on a cross for love of the world. Martin would only agree to the term *omnipotent* if one understands that the only real power in life is the power of agape, sacrificial love. Only this power is strong enough to die and in dying to rise again and to bring everything along with it. The Resurrection is not the reversal of the Crucifixion, it is the flowering of the Crucifixion.

✧ Martin believed that all religion of his day boiled down to two competing theologies: the "theology of glory" in which a person uses religion to secure his or her own advantage and power, and the "theology of the cross" in which a person gives himself or herself away for love. Meditate on the cross in your life.

✧ Ponder the paradoxes of life: without the cross, good things can become evil; with the cross, evil things can become good.

✧ Martin believed that Jesus' death on the cross was really our death. Can you see the old you—the egoism, the meanness, the prejudice—being put to death with Jesus? Are you willing to let the "old Adam" die? What would this mean in concrete terms?

✧ What is Martin's answer to the old questions: How can a loving God allow all this suffering? Why doesn't God do something? What is your answer?

✧ The church has tended to preach an "imperial deity," especially when it has said, "Outside the church there is no salvation." Is that imperial God compatible with a theology of the cross? How does the dying and rising God, the God of agape, relate to human beings of different faiths? How should we?

God's Word

For the message about the cross is foolishness to those who are perishing, but to us who are being saved it is the power of God. For it is written,
> "I will destroy the wisdom of the wise, and the
> discernment of the discerning I will thwart."

Where is the one who is wise? Where is the scribe? Where is the debater of this age? Has not God made foolish the wisdom of the world? For since, in the wisdom of God, the world did not know God through wisdom, God decided, through the foolishness of our proclamation, to save those who believe. For Jews demand signs and Greeks desire wisdom, but we proclaim Christ crucified, a stumbling block to Jews and foolishness to Gentiles, but to those who are the called, both Jews and Greeks, Christ the power of God and the wisdom of God. For God's foolishness is wiser than human wisdom, and God's weakness is stronger than human strength. (1 Corinthians 1:18–25)

Closing prayer:

Strengthen us so that the evil and misfortune of the world may not lead us into impatience, anger, revenge, or other wrongs. As we have vowed to you in Baptism, help us to renounce the lies, deceptions, false promises, and perjuries of the world, and all its good and evil. Enable us to remain true to this vow and to improve our lives daily. Amen. (Brokering, p. 37)

G·R·A·C·E

✧ Works Cited ✧

Bainton, Roland H. *Here I Stand: A Life of Martin Luther.* New York: New American Library, 1950.

Bernanos, Georges. *The Diary of a Country Priest.* New York: Macmillan, 1937.

Brokering, Herbert F., ed. *Luther's Prayers.* Minneapolis: Augsburg, 1994.

Brown, Norman O. *Life Against Death: The Psychoanalytical Meaning of History.* New York: Vintage Books, a division of Random House, 1959.

Dillenberger, John, ed. *Martin Luther: Selections from His Writings.* Garden City, NY: Anchor Books, Doubleday and Company, 1961.

Doberstein, John W., ed. *Minister's Prayer Book: An Order of Prayers and Readings.* Philadelphia: Fortress Press, n.d.

Dostoevsky, Fyodor. *Crime and Punishment.* New York: Bantam Books, 1959.

Elert, Werner. *The Structure of Lutheranism.* Vol. 1, *The Theology and Philosophy of Life of Lutheranism, Especially in the Sixteenth and Seventeenth Centuries.* Saint Louis: Concordia, 1962.

Empie, Paul C., T. Austin Murphy, and Joseph A. Burgess, eds. *Teaching Authority and Infallibility in the Church: Lutherans and Catholics in Dialogue VI.* Minneapolis: Augsburg, 1978.

Fischer, Robert H. *Luther.* Philadelphia: Lutheran Church Press, 1966.

Forell, George W., ed. *Luther's Works.* Vol. 32, *Career of the Reformer II.* Philadelphia: Muhlenberg Press, 1958.

Gritsch, Eric W., and Robert W. Jenson. *Lutheranism: The Theological Movement and Its Confessional Writings*. Philadelphia: Fortress Press, 1976.

Johnson, Thomas H., ed. *The Poems of Emily Dickinson*. Cambridge, MA: Belknap Press of Harvard University Press, 1951.

Lutheran Church in America. *Lutheran Book of Worship*. Minneapolis: Augsburg, 1978.

Moltmann, Jurgen. *The Crucified God: The Cross of Christ As the Foundation and Criticism of Christian Theology*. New York: Harper and Row, 1974.

National Council of the Churches of Christ in the United States of America. New Revised Standard Version of the Bible. Division of Christian Education of the National Council of the Churches of Christ in the United States of America, 1989.

Nohl, Frederick. *Martin Luther: Hero of Faith*. Saint Louis: Concordia, 1962.

Pelikan, Jaroslav, ed. *Luther's Works*. Vol. 6, *Lectures on Genesis, Chapters 31–37*. Saint Louis: Concordia, 1970.

———. *Luther's Works*. Vol. 13, *Selected Psalms II*. Saint Louis: Concordia, 1956.

Plass, Ewald M., comp. *What Luther Says: An Anthology*. Vol. 1, *Absolution—Giving*. Saint Louis: Concordia, 1959.

Rusch, William G., and Jeffrey Gros, eds. *Deepening Communion: International Ecumenical Documents with Roman Catholic Participation*. Washington, DC: United States Catholic Conference, 1998.

Tappert, Theodore G. *The Book of Concord: The Confessions of the Evangelical Lutheran Church*. Philadelphia: Fortress Press, 1959.

Acknowledgments *(continued)*

The scriptural quotations in this book are from the New Revised Standard Version of the Bible. Copyright © 1989 by the Division of Christian Education of the National Council of the Churches of Christ in the United States of America. All rights reserved.

The prayers on pages 40, 52, 58, 64, 70, 77, 84, 90, 97, 104, 110, 116, 122, and 127 are from *Luther's Prayers,* edited by Herbert F. Brokering (Minneapolis: Augsburg, 1994), pages 67–68, 18, 85, 89, 11, 35, 77, 51, 83, 12, 94–95, 103, 78, and 37, respectively. Copyright © 1994 by Augsburg. Used by permission.

The poem by Emily Dickinson on page 75 is from *The Poems of Emily Dickinson,* edited by Thomas H. Johnson (Cambridge, MA: Belknap Press of Harvard University Press, 1951). Copyright © 1983 by the President and Fellows of Harvard College. Reprinted by permission of Harvard University Press.

Titles in the Companions for the Journey Series

Praying with Anthony of Padua
Praying with Benedict
Praying with C. S. Lewis
Praying with Catherine McAuley
Praying with Catherine of Siena
Praying with Clare of Assisi
Praying with Dominic
Praying with Dorothy Day
Praying with Elizabeth Seton
Praying with Francis of Assisi
Praying with Francis de Sales
Praying with Frédéric Ozanam
Praying with Hildegard of Bingen
Praying with Ignatius of Loyola
Praying with John Baptist de La Salle
Praying with John Cardinal Newman
Praying with John of the Cross
Praying with Julian of Norwich
Praying with Louise de Marillac
Praying with Martin Luther
Praying with Meister Eckhart
Praying with Pope John XXIII
Praying with Teresa of Ávila
Praying with Thérèse of Lisieux
Praying with Thomas Merton
Praying with Vincent de Paul

Order from your local religious bookstore or from

Saint Mary's Press
702 Terrace Heights
Winona MN 55987-1320
USA
1-800-533-8095